Hybrid Project Management

Hybrid Project Management

Using Agile with Traditional PM Methodologies to Succeed on Modern Projects

Mark Tolbert and Susan Parente

Hybrid Project Management: Using Agile with Traditional PM Methodologies to Succeed on Modern Projects

Cover image licensed by Ingram Image, StockPhotoSecrets.com

Cover and interior design by Exeter Premedia Services Private Ltd., Chennai, India

First published in 2020 by
Business Expert Press, LLC
222 East 46th Street, New York, NY 10017
www.businessexpertpress.com

ISBN-13: 978-1-95253-834-6 (paperback)
ISBN-13: 978-1-95253-835-3 (e-book)

Business Expert Press Portfolio and Project Management Collection

Collection ISSN: 2156-8189 (print)
Collection ISSN: 2156-8200 (electronic)

First edition: 2020

10 9 8 7 6 5 4 3 2 1

Printed in the United States of America.

Abstract

We live in a very interesting time. Compared to just a couple of decades ago, there is much more volatility today in our marketplaces, the level of competition is much greater, we are operating in global economy, working virtually is no longer an anomaly. Considering all of this, it's much more difficult for companies to survive. On the other hand, there are tremendous opportunities for companies if they are able to be innovative and resilient, they can come up the right set of products and services at the right time.

As project managers, we are helping our companies survive in this difficult landscape. We are "agents of change" and "drivers of change." We are key to helping our companies survive in this volatile, difficult world. The most important project management methodology today that will help us deal with this change and this volatility is Agile. I believe all project managers need to come up-to-speed with at least the core principles of Agile, and understand how and why this is so important. Another important aspect of an Agile approach is applying this with a virtual team. Virtual teams have become quite common out of necessity however; too often "Agilists" (or purists of one of the Agile methodologies) lecture that Agile can only be done in a colocated environment. This is no longer the reality; many of our clients are using a Hybrid Agile approach for virtual project teams. This is a necessity for many organizations, including those that have multiple headquarters, or even a small team which includes experts around the world, or are located just a few hours drive away. Virtual project teams are commonplace for modern day projects.

However, no one process or project management methodology fits all situations! Agile is not a panacea for all projects. We believe that many times our projects are large enough and complex enough that some parts of the project are best suited to using a predictive planning approach, and other parts are more suited to using Agile. As PMs, we need to be flexible, and wear multiple hats: no one process or methodology fits all situations; we need to mature and not just be a purist for one and only one approach. Don't be a strict Agile partisan who believes Scrum or Kanban or another

Agile methodology is superior in all situations (Susan has coined the term 'Scrumdamentalist' to describe this type of person), and don't be a "Process purist" who believes following a set of predictive planning processes guarantees success, and must be enforced religiously. There are both strengths and weaknesses in different approaches, and the more we are aware of these, the more effective we will be. We should be open to using "Hybrid approaches" that even include the traditional waterfall approach.

In this book, we will also explore several key risks frequently faced on projects, and how Agile can help us solve these problems. We will also address how and when a traditional project management approach using "Predictive planning" is more appropriate.

Key risks we will explore are:

1. Poor Scope definition – (the #1 risk on projects)! This usually stems from doing the requirements gathering process poorly:
   - missing requirements
   - misunderstand requirements
   - misunderstanding the complexity of requirements
   - missing key stakeholders, and not obtaining their requirements
2. Impossible constraints starting out, and instances where the customer/sponsor wants assurances these constraints will be met.
3. Allowing "Half-Baked Ideas" to survive
4. Poor communications

Other topics that will be explored are:

- How to implement a hybrid approach that employs both traditional approaches and Agile approaches.
- Virtual Agile Teams
- Can Agile be used successfully with Earned Value (EVM)?
- A Review of Version Six of the ***PMBOK® Guide***: Thoughts and Retrospective
- Initial thoughts on the exposure draft of Version Seven of the ***PMBOK® Guide***

Intended Audience and Benefits – All project managers, program managers and business executives. If you don't know much about Agile and Lean methodologies, or want to learn more, and also learn why Agile is so important in our world today, we will explain why. We will also argue that "hybrid approaches" are particularly critical today for successful project management.

Mark Tolbert, PMP, PMI-ACP
Susan Parente, PMP, PMI-RMP, PMI-ACP, PSM I, CSM, CSPO, SFC, CISSP, CRISC, RESILIA, ITIL, GCLP, MS Eng. Mgmt.

July 23, 2020

Keywords

agile project management; scrum; lean; extreme (xp); waterfall; predictive planning; hybrid project management; virtual project teams; risk management; earned value management (evm); pmi; *pmbok® guide*; virtual; virtual agile; colocated; team charter; trust; agile ethos

Mark: To my wife, Linda, and my three boys, David, Brian and Michael

Susan: To my husband, Dave Schwartz for all his support and for being a source of inspiration

Inspiration for the Cover

The lighthouse theme represents our view that both Agile and hybrid methods (where traditional approaches are combined with various Agile approaches) are a vehicle to light the path of project uncertainty which all PMs face today. We hope that this book will support you in reducing the risk you face with your projects and shine light on the risks you manage, so you are able to use the practices and principles of Agile along with traditional practices to achieve project success for your current and future projects.

Contents

Introduction

Over the past five years, I've made a number of presentations to the Washington, DC PMI Chapter (PMIWDC) concerning Agile Project Management, Hybrid Projects, and how we can effectively integrate traditional project management approaches with Agile approaches to solve real-world project problems. I have also made presentations to other local PMI® Chapters, the U.S. Census Bureau, and other government agencies on this topic. This short book combines the central ideas of these presentations.

Mark Tolbert

Acknowledgments

I have been teaching PMP® Prep classes for the last 11 years as well as Agile (PMI-ACP® Prep) classes for the last 4 years. I've added several sections to the book with key ideas from these programs that I think are especially important for project managers today. I've also been a volunteer with the PMIWDC for most of the last 25 years, and I've attended a lot of dinner meetings and listened to many great presentations. I've incorporated key favorite ideas from many of these presentations in this book, too.

Lastly, Susan Parente, Jason Vorenkamp, and Carl Pritchard have also provided excellent help reviewing the book and providing examples and extra material. Susan has also contributed a chapter on "Virtual Agile Teams," and Jason provided examples for the "Problem Areas for Agile." Carl provided excellent feedback and suggestions in a number of areas in the book. I am also indebted to Laurie Martin Roberts for all her great work editing and reviewing this book.

CHAPTER 1

Hybrid Projects: The Need to Be Open to Different Project Management Methodologies

Introduction

I think as project managers (PMs), we often get too wedded to one particular methodology, and we think that this one methodology has to be used in all situations. We become purists for this one approach. Perhaps the methodology is Scrum or Extreme Programming (XP), and we think that this is the modern solution for all projects, and can and should be used on all projects. We think waterfall and traditional approaches are a thing of the past, and only something our fathers once had to use. There are much better ways to do things today![1]

Perhaps it's the other way around. Maybe there's a particular methodology or set of processes that our program management office (PMO) insists must be used on all projects. For example, the PMO stipulates that for all projects, there must be a formally approved project charter that is issued by the sponsor before any work is started. Additionally, there

---

[1] This reminds me of my time as an HP systems engineer in the 1980s: I was a die-hard defender of HP3000s and the MPE operating system, and I couldn't see my way to say anything positive about the DEC VAX architecture or the IBM 360/370 architecture! Similarly, I'm a die-hard sports fan today, and a complete supporter of the Washington Nationals and Washington Capitals. I have a hard time thinking of good things to say about opposing teams! I should really learn to be more open-minded, yes?

must be a written, formally approved project management plan with a minimum of 18 component pieces including formally approved baselines. The scope baseline must include the scope statement, a WBS (work breakdown structure), and WBS dictionary. There must be "management plans" that define how work and processes will be done in all nine Knowledge Areas except Integration Management. This formal project management plan must be approved before the "execution phases" of the project are started. Therefore, we will do predictive planning and move through the phases of the project in a waterfall fashion. Furthermore, Earned Value Management (EVM) must always be used to measure our project's progress against the baselines. This is our culture, and the PMO requires that this approach and set of processes be followed on all projects.

But this is too limiting and too narrow-minded, is it not? We need to be more versatile and more open-minded. We need to recognize that no one methodology or process is perfect for all situations. Isn't it also the case that most of our projects are probably large enough and complex enough that parts of the project are very suitable for the tried-and-true traditional methods, or waterfall methods, and other parts require creativity and exploring requirements, so they are much more suitable to Agile? On a large, complex project, isn't it likely that some parts are "cookie-cutter," so to speak? These parts involve work-packages or items that we've done many times in the past, and we have very good historical records for these parts or work-packages. For these parts, we know in detail starting out exactly what the requirements are, and what the relative priorities are of the requirements. "The customer knows exactly what they want at the beginning." These historical records will allow us to obtain very good estimates of time and cost, and very good templates of different types of key documents that can be used in our project. Therefore, for these parts of the project, it will probably make sense to use predictive planning or a waterfall approach and also have a fully accountable PM[2] who

[2] Many people in the Agile community refer to this type of traditional PM who is fully accountable for the project, and who is the single focal point for the project - as a "command and control PM!" Obviously, that has negative connotations, and makes it sound if all such traditional PMs are micromanagers, and are quite dictatorial. Of course, that doesn't have to be the case at all.

is assigning all the work to the different team members. Perhaps many of these parts of the project will be subcontracted out to external vendors, and the work will be performed under a fixed-price contract. We must have all the I's dotted and the T's crossed! There is an extensive Statement of Work (SOW), and again, it will make most sense to use the traditional approach.

For these "cookie-cutter projects" or "cookie-cutter parts of projects," why does it make a lot of sense to use predictive planning, a waterfall approach, and have the traditional, fully accountable PM? Because it is much less expensive and far more efficient to do so! Use the "KISS" principle: "Keep It Simple Stupid!" or "Occam's Razor"—"Don't multiply entities beyond necessity." With Agile, we want to have a team made up of 5 to 10 senior, dedicated members. That's going to be very expensive in most cases. Furthermore, ideally, we want them to be colocated. That's also going to be very tough to do in many cases today in our modern project world and also very expensive. In the situation where we know exactly what is needed starting out in the project, this is not necessary. We can go with the traditional predictive planning model, which is much leaner and more efficient, and accomplish our goals in the same amount of time and for far less money.

Many of the projects I've worked on in my career at Hewlett-Packard were of this nature. These were "logistics projects"—data center relocations or large "rollouts" as we called them. We were refreshing the client PCs and other supporting servers for a large customer at numerous office sites, we had done these types of projects many times before, and we had very good historical records that gave us excellent estimates of time and cost.[3] So it did make sense to have a traditional PM, who was totally

---

[3] Does that mean that these types of projects were simpler and easier? Not at all. Everything in the project needed to run like clockwork, and the customer was often very demanding. There was no room for errors or mistakes. As always, there was tremendous pressure to communicate very well concerning project commitments: Communicate completely and accurately to the customer and to other key stakeholders. For this type of project, the old saying especially applies, "the devil is in the details." We had to be sure we were on the same page with the customer and the other stakeholders.

accountable for the project, doing predictive planning, and handing out all the parts of the plans of the project to the different team members and subcontractors. These team members were working part-time on the project and were multitasking between a number of projects.

Also, the resources on my projects were often spread out over a large geography, so it would be impractical to have them colocated. That would also increase the cost and in most cases would not be something that management was readily agreeable to. Again, in my project world, we were using virtual teams spread out over a large geography in almost all cases, and the team members and subcontractors were working on multiple projects at the same time.

The Landscape for Projects Today

However, I think the types of projects most of us are dealing with today are much different than what I just described. How would you describe our world today for project management? What good adjectives or descriptive phrases would you use to describe this world that we find ourselves in? I think it's a more difficult, more challenging world today than it was for PMs just a couple of decades ago. The pace of change has increased in amazing ways. Some catchphrases that seem to apply to our world today are:

- "Make dust or eat dust!"
- "If you are standing still, you are falling behind!"
- "The only constant is change!" (This is from 500 BC—Ancient Greek philosophy—Heraclitus!)
- Companies are dealing with global marketplaces, and more competition than ever.
- Customers are very demanding, very fickle.
- The need to adapt to changing marketplace conditions is greater than ever.
- "Change or Die!"

We are dealing with a much tougher competitive landscape today—we will say more about that momentarily—but change is occurring much more quickly than it ever did before, our customers are more demanding than ever, they're more fickle, and, therefore, it's tougher for companies today. They have to constantly find new products, new services, and new solutions that respond to the new demands of their customers. They must adapt to the changing landscape of what customers are looking for. I think Jeff Sutherland sums it up best in his book, *Scrum: The Art of Doing Twice the Work in Half the Time*. He simply says, "Change or die!"

I think Thomas Friedman, in several of his more recent books, explains very well how and why we have reached this new age: an age of tremendous change and increased competition. He terms this new age an "Age of Accelerations." He has written three books that all address this topic: the first book was *The World Is Flat*, the second book *That Used to Be Us: How America Fell Behind in the World It Invented* (a fairly scary and eye-opening book for those of us who live in the United States), and the third book *Thank You for Being Late*. Each book builds on the themes and key points made in the preceding books. Friedman points out there were two things that happened together over two decades ago in the early 1990s. First, it was the breakup of the Soviet Union in the late 1980s that ushered in a new era of globalization in the early 1990s. That brought new countries into our capitalist marketplaces, and this raised the bar of competition in very significant ways. Of course, we're talking about China, but also India, and many other countries.

Something else also happened at the same time in the early 1990s that was a tremendous game changer. Of course, that was the advent of the Internet, and the Internet has changed almost everything about how we live, how we play, and how we do business and work. Global teams can collaborate on work, share documents, and communicate in very creative and new ways.

Here is another type of example of how the Internet has changed our world. Imagine that a group of young entrepreneurs has come together with an idea for a new business solution. The team is confident this business solution is going to have a lot of appeal to people and make a big impact. They don't need the old-fashioned brick-and-mortar manufacturing operation to produce the products they are envisioning—they can outsource that. For advertising and marketing, they can outsource that too. They can even find very creative ways to get financing to provide the necessary funding for this opportunity. Bottom line, it's much easier today for people to form new companies to go after opportunities, and people are doing exactly that today. This has raised the level of competition in major ways. A number of different writers say that the Internet has brought about as profound a change in our world as the Gutenberg printing press did in the 15th century. So, in short, we're living in this age of accelerations with tremendous change and a heightened level of competition.

Why does this matter to us as PMs? Why do we care about all this volatility, difficult marketplaces, and the challenges our companies are facing? Of course, it's simply because we are helping our companies survive in these difficult times. We are managing change for them, and we are helping our companies create the new products and solutions that will resonate with customers. We are drivers of change in this new world! Therefore, our companies need us to be very good at managing projects and to be up-to-speed with the latest methodologies. So, what project management methodology is best suited for coping with change and handling volatility? Of course, that's an easy answer; the answer is Agile! But we shouldn't discard the tried and true—the traditional waterfall approaches. As we'll see, this methodology also has an important role in many projects. We need to be open-minded and know when and where to use the different approaches and the strengths and weaknesses of the different approaches.

The Roots of Modern Project Management and the Case for Traditional Project Management

From what industry did project management arise and who wrote the first books and anthologies on project management? It was the construction and engineering industry that provided the foundations of our modern project management practices. The first authors of college textbooks on project management were engineering professors: people like Clelland and King (1968) and Harold Kerzner (1979).

Some people might say that modern project management starts with Henry Gantt and Gantt charts in 1910. These were used successfully with the Hoover Dam project in the 1930s. Other people point to the 1950s with the advent of Program Evaluation and Review Technique (PERT), which was used with the Navy Polaris Submarine program, and with critical path method (CPM), devised in the late 1950s at DuPont. Also, much of the traditional project management approach comes to us from the 1960s and the Department of Defense (DoD). Much of what we teach in our Project Management Professional (PMP®) Prep classes is based on the core principals developed in DoD, especially EVM and the WBS. The WBS is a key part of Earned Value (EV) and is very close to the heart of the traditional PM. The WBS drives all planning, or is the "cornerstone of all planning." It drives scheduling, cost estimating, and budgeting, determining quality acceptance values, resource estimating, identifying risks, and deciding what we want to outsource. Of course, we also have the 100 percent rule: "100 percent of the project must be in the WBS! If it's not in the WBS, it's not in the project!"

What is the lifecycle model that is very closely tied to traditional project management? The "waterfall lifecycle approach" and the use of predictive planning. This model entails:

- Performing exhaustive, detailed planning for all phases of the project at the beginning ("The devil is in the details!"). Therefore, don't leave any stones unturned; figure out all requirements, in detail, in your planning phases at the beginning of the project. Plan everything so well from the beginning that change won't be needed! As Harold Kerzner says in his textbook on project management,[4] do planning so well that scope changes are kept to a minimum.
- Hierarchically decomposing your original business requirements and functional requirements to a very detailed level using a WBS.
- Obtaining accurate, detailed estimates for time and cost at the work-package level using techniques such as bottom-up estimating, parametric estimating, and PERT three-point estimating.

[4] *Project Management—A Systems Approach to Planning, Scheduling, and Controlling* by Harold Kerzner, Ph.D., p. 6.

- Measuring performance during the project using EVM.
- Measuring performance against all three baselines (scope, schedule, and cost) using EVM, and using *Quantitative Risk Analysis* techniques to more accurately define contingency reserves to include in the cost baseline and schedule baseline.

If you're building a new bridge or building, you probably want to use this waterfall approach. You had better get very detailed, accurate blueprints created before you start construction. Then, you will need very accurate baselines with which to measure your performance. Detailed blueprints (and a WBS) will allow you to create an accurate schedule and budget, so you can measure your performance against time and cost. Ideally, you will use EVM to do this. In EVM, they like to say, "To do project management properly, you need to have *defined scope.*" If you have this, you can define all three key baselines: scope, schedule, and cost.

EVM really works hand-in-hand with traditional project management and a waterfall approach. For EVM to work, we need to have very accurate baselines and a very accurate BAC (budget at completion). In an excellent book on EV written by Fleming and Koppelman, *Simple Earned Value on All Projects—(Simplified Translations of the 27 EVM Criteria),* they state the most important of all the 27 criteria is the very first one. Here is their translation:

Step 1: To the extent possible, you must define the full scope of the project.—(Equates to EVM Criterion #1)

- This is perhaps the most important requirement for implementing earned value, and perhaps the most difficult to achieve. Management of certain types of projects, notably software, often give up at this point and refuse to go further. They often relinquish (p. 160).

  They go further on p. 178:
- The first group of criteria deals with the requirement for any new project to be completely defined, and planned, prior to starting performance of the work. Today, we would typically call this effort defining the scope of the project. Think about

> it: Earned Value Measurement cannot take place without some definition of what constitutes 100 percent of the project.

Why is it so crucial in construction and engineering to first obtain the full scope of the entire project—all the requirements spelled out in detail—before we start construction? The answer is pretty obvious. If there's a mistake in our blueprints and construction begins; and, if the mistake in the blueprints is not discovered until weeks have gone by, and a lot of construction work has been done, all that engineering and construction work might have to be torn up and redone. Of course, that is going to be very, very expensive. Someone's probably going to lose their job!

My youngest son, Michael, works for a design/build mechanical firm using 3D CAD (computer-aided design). He's creating the blueprints for all the mechanical and plumbing work in large high-rise apartment buildings. He's told me, "Dad, if my blueprints for the mechanical and plumbing design in the building are off by even a quarter of an inch, then there will be hell to pay." Predictive planning must be done, and every detail nailed down, too. Michael's BIM (Building Information Modeling) team must coordinate everything at the start of a construction project to collaborate with the engineering team and make sure each floor of the building is "clash free" (virtually) before construction starts. This is necessary to avoid expensive change orders that could potentially happen in the field. For example, suppose the BIM team didn't realize there was a 24 × 48 beam blocking a 22 × 14 duct going into the lobby area! "The Devil is in the details!"

Is predictive planning and this attention to detail only critical in construction and engineering projects where the cost of change once we started construction could be very, very high? If we're doing a software application, and the change will just involve moving bits around and recompiling programs, do we still have the same urgency to get all our requirements totally correct at the beginning? Is it even possible to do that?

On construction projects, it's usually the case that the customer knows much more precisely what they want going into the project than they would on a typical software project, or "knowledge work" project. Perhaps it is a new office building. In most cases, the customer will know exactly what they can afford, when the building needs to be completed, and the other requirements: number of offices, conference rooms, size of the lobby area, number of floors and footprint, power and HVAC requirements, networking requirements, architectural style, and so on. The architect will create detailed blueprints and models that the customer will review and accept before construction begins. Or … perhaps it's a home kitchen remodeling project. The key stakeholder—the wife—will choose exactly what appliances she wants, the cabinets, and counter-tops. Perhaps a general contractor will be engaged, and after design meetings with the homeowners, they will create blueprints or CAD drawings of the new kitchen that the homeowners will accept or modify. Again, the customer will determine, in detail, all the requirements before the "demolition" and "remodeling" phases begin. Therefore, on these types of projects, it's a much more straightforward process to obtain all the requirements upfront at the beginning of the project.

These types of projects are much more conducive to using a fixed-price contract. Once given the detailed requirements, the contractor will be able to determine their costs precisely and generate a fixed-price bid. (Fixed-price contracts and other contracts are presented in more detail in Chapter 2—"Agile Contracts: Can Agile Be Used with Fixed-Price Contracts?")

Risk #1: The Number One Risk on Projects!

There are several other reasons the traditional "waterfall" methodology often makes sense. What is the principal cause of failure on projects and, therefore, our "Number One Risk?" It's having a poorly written scope statement: a vague, ambiguous scope statement. If we allow that to happen, there will be no hope for this project. In a key process—*Validate Scope*—defined in the Scope Management KA, *Project Management Body of Knowledge* (*PMBOK® Guide*),[5] we bring in the customer to inspect deliverables that we've created and obtain their formal acceptance. If our scope statement is vague or ambiguous, and the acceptance criteria in

---

[5] Project Management Institute, *A Guide to the Project Management Body of Knowledge,* Sixth Edition, Project Management Institute, Inc., 2017.

the scope statement are poorly written—not "SMART"—*s*pecific, *m*easurable, *a*greed, *r*ealistic, and *t*imebound—how is this meeting with the customer going to go? Of course, not well at all! What are we likely to hear? "I'm sorry, but this isn't exactly what I'm looking for." ... and, of course ... "Weren't you listening? I absolutely need to have these other requirements too!" ... etc. And, if our scope statement is vague or ambiguous and if the acceptance criteria for this deliverable were poorly written, then we're going to have to add in these extra requirements at our own expense. This leads to what we hate most—Scope Creep![6] Scope Creep is "The uncontrolled expansion of project scope or product scope without making adjustments to time, cost and resources,"[7] which leads to schedule delays, budget overruns, customer satisfaction issues, and senior management satisfaction issues with the project. And, very likely, a new PM! Therefore, follow all the *PMBOK® Guide* planning processes in Scope Management very well: *Plan Scope Management; Collect Requirements; Define Scope; Create WBS.* Following these processes ensures you are on the same page with the customer; all the requirements have been captured and the acceptance criteria for the deliverables are "SMART."

This leads us to a discussion of why the job of the PM is a very difficult job. I like to say, "Project management is not for sissies!" Project management is essentially all about people skills or soft skills. It is not really about understanding the technical intricacies of scheduling tools like Microsoft Project, Primavera, or Artemis (e.g., understanding how to do a forward pass and backward pass; understanding the difference between total float and free float). It is not about understanding the arcane tools and techniques mentioned for *Quantitative Risk Analysis:* EMV (expected monetary value) or Monte Carlo simulation or decision trees or a sensitivity analysis. It is not about the "IQ (Intellectual Quotient) part of the equation"; it is about the "EQ (Emotional Quotient) part of the equation" or

---

[6] To be technically correct, "Scope Creep" is not a risk, it's the effect or outcome if we do not handle risks in Scope Management well. Once a risk occurs, it's no longer a risk; it's an "issue." Risks are all about uncertainty and probability.

[7] Project Management Institute, *A Guide to the Project Management Body of Knowledge, (PMBOK® Guide),* Sixth Edition, Project Management Institute, 2017, Page 168.

emotional intelligence. What is the key part of emotional intelligence or the key part of people skills and soft skills? Clearly, the answer is good communication skills. What is the essence of having good communication skills? (Something that technical people like me have a lot of difficulty with!) Good listening skills. All good communicators are necessarily very good listeners.

In the *PMBOK® Guide*, PMI® does not put any priorities on the processes in the different Knowledge Areas. But I will go out on a limb and do that! I think the highest priority Knowledge Areas are *Scope Management; Communications Management; and Stakeholder Management.* Success on our projects directly depends on how well we perform key processes in these Knowledge Areas, and these Knowledge Areas all really overlap one another (Figure 1.1).

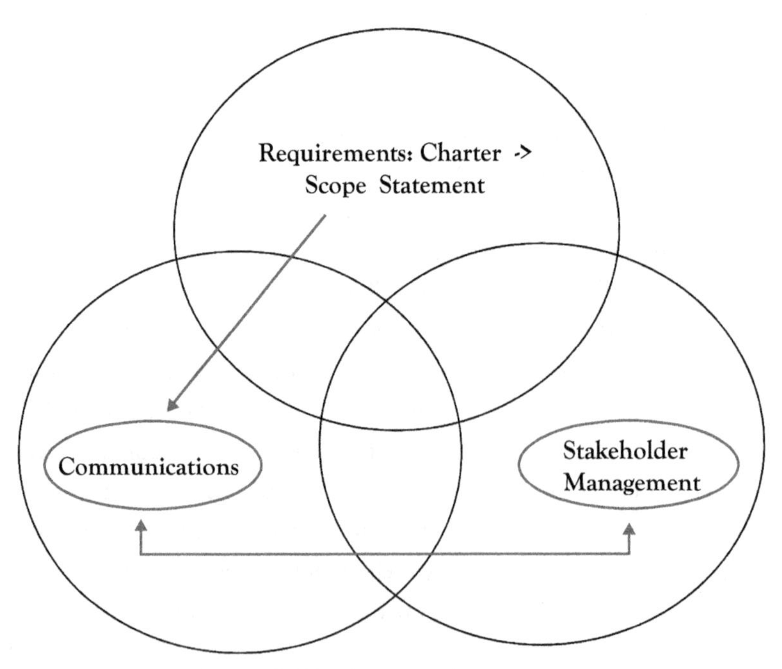

Figure 1.1 Foundational KAs (processes)

1. As we said, our principal risk involves doing Scope Management well and this starts with doing the requirements gathering process well.
   - *Don't miss any requirements.*
   - *Don't misunderstand the requirements.*

- *Don't misunderstand the complexity of the requirements: Decompose requirements properly.*
- *Don't miss any key stakeholders in obtaining requirements.*

2. Successfully obtaining requirements involves communicating very well with the customer and other key stakeholders. This includes listening! Follow well-accepted practices like JAD (joint application design) and QFD (quality function deployment). In essence, get those engineers out of their offices to go meet with the customer. Have productive conversations with the customer to truly understand what they are seeking. Don't assume that we know best what the customer really wants! Get out of our offices, follow the customer around to see what they're really needing. Even better, try out their job for part of the day, so we truly understand what they need.
3. Let's assume that we do the requirements gathering process very well; we erred on the side of inclusiveness, we've done brainstorming, we've been creative, and we correctly captured all the different stakeholder requirements. Are we now in good shape? Are we going to be successful? No, not necessarily! This is where the hard part of project management comes in. Are the stakeholders all in agreement for the requirements for the project? Of course not! The requirements they want are all over the map. They have different needs and different wants. Somehow, someway, we have to get them onto the same page. If we don't do that, this project is surely going to fail, and who's going to take the blame? Not these stakeholders who are giving us all these inconsistent requirements. No, you will take the blame (the PM).

Many of the PMP® Prep books completely misunderstand this key point about what is happening as we move from *Collect Requirements* to *Define Scope.* The *PMBOK® Guide* doesn't even emphasize this enough! Many people think that as we move into *Define Scope,* we are just digging into more and more detail. That is not the key purpose of *Define Scope.* No, the key purpose is to get everyone onto the same page; "define boundaries," and "define exclusions." This is the hard part of project management. No matter what powers we have as PMs—we could be that very empowered PM in a strong matrix organization that we assume is the default for the PMP®

exam—we will never have enough power to legislate what will be in scope and what will not be in scope. No matter how powerful we are, we are dealing with stakeholders who are much more powerful than we are: the sponsor and other senior managers in our own organization, the customer, even stakeholders in other organizations (e.g., federal regulatory organizations).

Nonetheless, for this project to succeed, we must get everybody onto the same page; we must define the boundaries and the exclusions for the project. If this doesn't happen, this project will fail. I've been to many dinner meetings for the Washington, DC PMI® Chapter (PMIWDC) over the past 20+ years, and I've heard many excellent presentations about projects where things went dreadfully wrong. In almost all cases (F-22, Affordable Healthcare Act website project, etc.), these projects failed because this problem was not correctly handled. So, we must obtain requirements correctly and create a well-written scope statement with SMART acceptance criteria. To do that, we must do communications very well, but we must also do *Stakeholder Management* very well to define these boundaries and exclusions.

By the way, who has most of the risk in this situation? The sponsor? The customer? The senior managers who gave us the incompatible requirements? No, the PM has the risk! If we fail to get everyone on the same page and proceed trying to run this project, it is surely going to fail. When that happens, who will take the blame, and who will be looking for a new job? We will: the PM!

4. Criterion number one, defined in the most current EVM specification, is directly addressing this point, "to the extent possible you must define the full scope of the project!"

But, let's suppose we do all this correctly; we do correctly follow the planning processes in Scope Management defined in the *PMBOK® Guide*, we do get boundaries and exclusions defined, and do get everyone "onto the same page." Does that now guarantee success for the project? No, it does not!

The Case for Agile

Suppose the customer doesn't know exactly what they want at the beginning of the project, and they want a new solution created for them. They know high-level business requirements or functional requirements, but they don't know the exact detailed engineering solution. That needs to be explored and discovered, and it's understood there's going to be some trial and error in discovering the best engineering solution. But, instead of using an iterative approach, we follow the guidance of Fleming and Koppelman, and we do our best at the beginning of the project to uncover in a detailed way all the scope requirements. It is 1978, and we are using a waterfall approach for developing this application. We are going to do predictive planning! (Waterfall approaches using "predictive planning" were typically used for developing software applications in the 1970s and 1980s. Some people are still using this type of approach for software applications today!) A simplified view of the waterfall lifecycle model we used might look like the one in Figure 1.2.

We spent several months interviewing all the different stakeholders on the project, making sure that we didn't miss anyone or leave anyone out. We thoroughly captured all of their requirements for this new application: layouts of reports they wanted to see, the graphical user interface (GUI) for input screens, file layouts of other input files, expected response times and throughput times, and other details. We created the user

Organize the project in phases. Phases are often organized in a sequential manner (or "Waterfall" structure.)

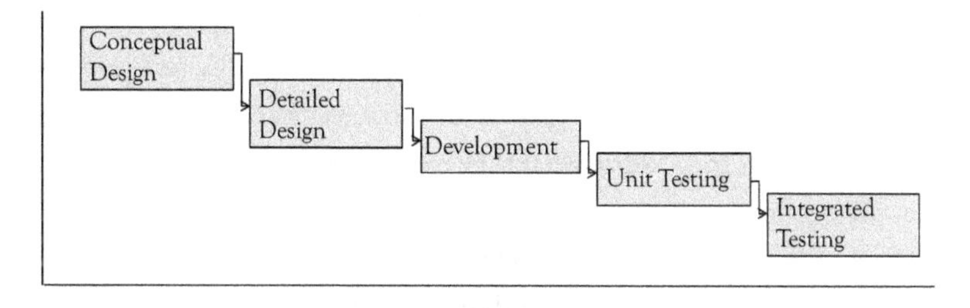

Phases

Figure 1.2 Traditional project lifecycle structure

requirements documentation (the functional specification). We obtained all the necessary approvals, and had a bow tied around these documents.

We then turned over these documents to the systems analysts, who did the detailed design. They hierarchically decomposed the application: from the application down to programs, from the programs down to modules, from modules down to subroutines, and from subroutines down to functions, and so forth. They defined the interfaces between each level and the parameters that would be passed. They defined all the file layouts. This also took several months to accomplish. Again, the necessary approvals were obtained on the subsystem specification, or the system architecture document. Now, the system architecture documentation was turned over to the Cobol and Fortran programmers, who did the coding and development. How long did that take? An average application at the time of 1978 was usually more than 100,000 lines of code, and it typically took more than a year to do all the coding and unit testing. Then the programmers brought all their code together to do integrated testing, and this could also take more than a month or two.

Finally, that glorious day arrived: UAT! (User acceptance testing). How did UAT go? Not well at all! Why? Well, how long was it before the customer really got to see the running application? It was 18 months or longer! What's happened in that year and a half? The world has changed! By the time of UAT, there were much better ways to do things; better ways to index records to provide faster response times; and better GUIs and screen designs for inputting data and reviewing data. The customer wanted these new technologies, and was not happy with an application that had been designed 18 months or more earlier. Even more fundamentally, it's not until the customer uses the application, sees real response times and throughput times, plays with the screens and sees how everything works that they realize what they really needed in the first place. So, they are not happy at all!

Therefore, Fleming and Koppelman were wrong! It's not that as software PMs we gave up too soon and didn't try hard enough to determine the real requirements the customer needed; it just wasn't possible to do that. The world was changing too quickly, and at the time of obtaining the user requirements, we could not see, and the customer could not see, how things would change and what detailed engineering solution would

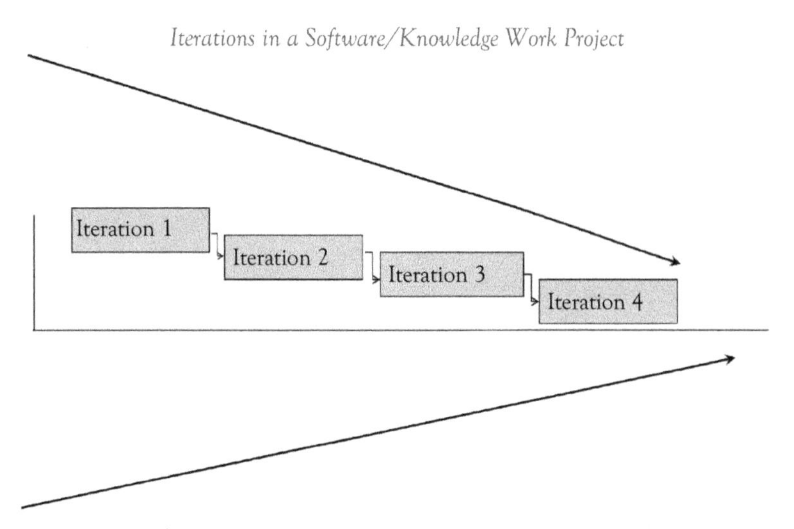

Figure 1.3 The "Cone of Uncertainty"

work best. In our world today—Tom Friedman's "*Age of Accelerations*"—as PMs, we are dealing much more with the *"Cone of Uncertainty"* (Figure 1.3).

In the first iterations of the project, it's impossible to predict accurately exactly what detailed design solution will work best for the project at its end-date—perhaps one year out, or longer. The world is changing very quickly, and new technologies and solutions will become available, and these will likely change the final engineering solution the team decides upon. It's also impossible at the beginning to get accurate forecasts of time and cost for the entire project (or release). Our job is to discover and explore what will work best. It's implied that in this "Age of Accelerations" and very volatile requirements, we are under much more pressure to deliver quickly, and there are tight schedule constraints. We need the team of 5 to 10 senior, colocated, "generalizing specialists" to help us meet these tight schedule constraints.

So, what is the best way to handle these types of situations? For software applications or "knowledge work" projects based on intellectual work and design work, the best approach is to do things iteratively; use Agile. In very short iterations—one to four weeks—get a subset of the application out to the customer, and let them kick the tires so to speak, and find out what has value and what does not. The Agile lifecycle is going to look as given in Figure 1.4.

"Initiation"	Release Planning	Iteration 1	Iteration 2	Iteration 3
Create Charter Create Backlog High-level estimates Create Roadmap Story Maps	Story Estimating Planning Poker Build Release Plan	Sprint Planning Development Unit Testing Integrated Testing Sprint Review/ Demo. Retrospective	Sprint Planning Development Unit Testing Integrated Testing Sprint Review/ Demo. Retrospective	Sprint Planning Development Unit Testing → Integrated Testing Sprint Review/ Demo. Retrospective

Figure 1.4 Agile lifecycle

Once we get through the initiation phase and the release planning phase, and into the "development iterations," each development iteration is a vertical slice of the entire project, and aspects of all phases are used in each development iteration. (Also, it goes without saying that all five process groups are used in each iteration.) In each development iteration, we will do planning, we will execute against those plans to create "product increment"—something empirical and tangible (usually a prototype of some deliverable, but not a throwaway prototype) and something that can go into production. In each development iteration, we will also do testing and quality control (QC) and get acceptance from the product owner and/or customer.

A key aspect of what happens using Agile approaches and doing things iteratively is that we are using Lean. Lean is a core part of all the different Agile methodologies. With Lean, we are "grooming the value chain" and "identifying fast failures" (or identifying failures fast). When we go to obtain requirements from our customers, what are they likely to give us? Everything! Really! Everything under the sun remotely imagined for this project. And … everything is priority one! Doesn't the federal government do this in most of their requests for proposals (RFPs)? As I remember things, for a large federal IT procurement RFP in the 1990s—TAC4—there was so much in the RFP that even a huge company like mine (Hewlett-Packard) could not meet all the requirements on our own. We had to find vendors and subcontractors, who could fill the gaps of what we could not provide to have any hope of winning this opportunity. Was the federal government likely to use all these requirements? Never!

In one Standish survey of several years ago, it was quoted that "65% of the requirements the customer thinks they absolutely have to have will never be used." There is some controversy about how the Standish group came up with this 65 percent number, but another way of viewing the situation that is widely accepted is another version of Pareto's law. For Quality Management, all my PMP® Prep students know that Pareto's law is "80 percent of the problems come from 20 percent of the causes." In sales, Pareto's law is "80 percent of your orders come from 20 percent of your customers." In requirements, Pareto's law is "80 percent of the customer's need comes from 20 percent of the requirements." Therefore, using Agile, we will go after this 20 percent of the requirements in our first iterations. Very quickly we will get something out to the customer that is empirical and tangible, and demonstrates this "product increment" to them. We will find out what has value and what does not. If features we've included in the product turn out not to have value, then we will delete these from the "backlog." We won't invest in them further; we won't have to do further integrated testing, we won't have to do as much documentation, and therefore, we will save time and we will save money. We will keep "grooming the value chain" using Lean.

Creating something that's empirical and tangible, and then demonstrating this to the product owner and the customer, also has tremendous value. It is far more valuable to show them something empirical, than just have them review large documents of specifications. In a wonderful quote from Doug DeCarlo in his excellent book, *Extreme Project Management,* he says, "If a picture is worth a thousand words, a prototype is worth a thousand pictures." The product increment we are creating in each iteration is very similar to a prototype, but it is not just a model, or a mockup of the deliverable that will be thrown away. What we are creating is a subset of the overall application or solution, but it is something that will go into production.

In *Scrum: The Art of Doing Twice the Work in Half the Time,*[8] Sutherland gives us a number of real-world examples of the benefits of Agile. One of these case examples was from 2006 and involved Medco.[9] At that time Medco was the world's largest online pharmacy.

---

[8] Jeff Sutherland is one of the coauthors of Scrum along with Ken Schwaber.

[9] *Scrum: The Art of Doing Twice the Work in Half the Time* by Jeff Sutherland, J.J. Sutherland p. 111.

Here are some key bullet points from this case example:
Medco, 2006

- At the time, Medco was a Fortune 100 Firm: world's largest online pharmacy.
- Medco planned to rollout a new online pharmacy that would link patients with a pharmacist who would review all their different prescriptions and ensure there were no conflicts. Furthermore, they would guarantee a significant cost savings for patients moving to this online pharmacy.
- The CEO had checked with the IT management team and received assurances this was technically feasible, but he did not get any details on how long it would take!
- He promised Wall Street that this new online pharmacy capability would be available in one year, by July 7, 2007!
- Wall Street loved this entire idea, and Medco's stock took a very nice jump upwards.
- However, the people who had to implement this capability did not learn they would be going forward with the massive project until after the CEO had made the commitment to Wall Street! But the challenges to implement this were immense!
- Much of the software the company relied upon to direct on-site robots was badly outdated.
- In Medco's five gargantuan plants, filled with 4,000 pharmacists processing prescriptions, robots whizzed about pulling pills while other robots handled packaging and mailing, and all those systems had to talk to one another with 100 percent accuracy, or someone would die!
- It took the company six months to figure out they couldn't do it on time.
- In the *best-case* scenario, it would be a year late!
- They thought they could plan everything ahead of time. They spent months of effort making a detailed project management plan with pretty charts. This was all fiction!

- There were reams of paper outlining requirements, compliance, all sorts of reports, and quality assurance (QA). The stack of requirements documentation was two feet tall.
- There were so many people involved and at loggerheads that everything was deadlocked.
- So, they used the Scrum process to pull out the most essential requirements (backlog items).
- They wrote all these items down on sticky notes, plastering the walls with hundreds and hundreds of sticky notes. (This process of pulling out the minimum viable product items and writing them down on sticky notes took several hours.)
- Then, they conducted a high-level estimation of the backlog items.
- And, finally, "What do we need to do first?" Prioritize the work—what is the "20 percent of the requirements that would fulfill 80 percent of the need?"
- Bottom line—Medco met their July 2007 date!

I believe many Agilists miss the key point of using Lean. They think the key purpose of using Lean with Agile methodologies is eliminating and reducing waste. Here are the classic seven key types of waste (from Poppendieck) that we focus on eliminating:

- Partially done work
- Extra processes
- Extra features
- Task switching
- Waiting
- Motion
- Defects

Eliminating this type of waste is important, but this is not the key thing we are achieving using Lean. As we are seeing in this Medco example, the most important benefit of using Lean for our projects, today, is identifying the 20 percent of the requirements that will provide 80 percent of the customer's need and continuously grooming the value chain. We are going to save time and money if we do this right. Involving the customer on a much more frequent basis to review what the team is creating is also instrumental to achieving this goal. If we use Lean properly, we are going to create something of higher value as we iteratively move through the project than if we used a predictive planning approach to figure out everything, in detail, at the beginning. Starting out, we can't predict exactly what it is we will achieve at the end of the project, or at the end of the release, but if we use Lean properly, it will be of higher value!

At a College of Performance Management (CPM) meeting I attended a couple of years ago (this was a meeting attended by more than 50 senior EVM program managers), the attendees were trying to solve the problem of how they could use Agile effectively with their EVM programs. The federal government was demanding that they do this, and frankly, the program managers were scratching their heads and wondering how and why they should do this. They could see the benefits of running daily standup meetings in many of their projects, and using burndown charts and Kanban Boards, but from my vantage point, they were missing the whole point of why we use Agile. It's really about reaping the benefits of using Lean, especially for software and "knowledge work" projects. As I'll discuss further, if we do this right, we can achieve a 300 percent or greater improvement in our productivity! After the meeting, in the "social networking part" of the meeting, I tried to explain this to one of the EVM program managers, and he looked at me incredulously and said something to the effect that I was an Agile zealot. (I'll leave out his exact phrasing!) I replied back, "No, I'm really not. I'm an enthusiastic hybrid zealot!" (Again, my exact words will be omitted!)[10]

In Agile, we're actually improving and speeding up the classic plan-do-check-act (PDCA) loop. The PDCA loop was given to us by Walter Shewhart and W. Edwards Deming. (Shewhart originated this idea in 1939, and Deming added on more thought for its use in 1950.) The PDCA

[10] For another example of how Agile allows to quickly identify the 20 percent of the requirements that will meet 80 percent of the customer's need in the first iterations of a project, see the section in Agile Contracts on "Money for Nothing and Change for Free" contracts.

loop has become the foundation for the best accepted practices in Quality Management for how to achieve continuous improvement, or Kaizen, on our projects. ("Kaizen" is the Japanese term for continuous improvement. "Kai" is to alter or to change; "Zen" is to improve.) The idea is to "Make small incremental, continuous improvements in all aspects of your project; your products, your plans and documents, and even your processes. Don't try to solve everything at once; don't try to 'boil the ocean'; do things incrementally and iteratively." Of course, this shouldn't only be applied to projects; it applies to both projects and operations. It applies to all steps in the entire product lifecycle. In fact, the PDCA loop and Lean and the Toyota Production System have their origin in manufacturing processes and operational processes. The best of the modern proprietary quality methodologies—Six Sigma, Toyota Production System—Lean, Capability Maturity Model Integration (CMMI), Just-in-Time (JIT), ISO-9000 (International Organization of Standardization)—are focused on improving operational and manufacturing processes, and using the PDCA loop is emphasized in all these proprietary methodologies.

Lean later evolved into the Lean Software Development movement as a subculture of the Agile movement in the early 2000s. But, interestingly, in the *PMBOK® Guide*, for determining the business case for the project, and in the Cost Management chapter, doing "lifecycle costing" has always been emphasized. Thus, this is a part of traditional project management. The idea is, as you do your project, don't take a short-range view. Don't make decisions that save money and costs for the project lifecycle where such decisions could lower quality on the product or make it hard to maintain the product in operations and, therefore, hurt the company in the long term. Take the long-term view. Design the product for the long run, so it is easy and practical to maintain and has the right level of quality (so it doesn't have to be repaired frequently!) to protect the company into the future. Therefore, as we do our projects, protect the entire product lifecycle. Design in the right QC processes, make sure the project is consistent with the company's quality policies and methodologies, and that process improvement processes have been designed into the project. Use the best-quality processes inside the project itself.

In Agile, we're speeding up this PDCA loop in some very important ways. On a classic software development project (circa 1978!), how often did we meet with the customer? Not very often! We met with them at the beginning of the project to obtain user requirements and to write the functional specification, and then, we went away for almost two years to develop the application. It wasn't until UAT—often times two years after the start—when the customer saw the real, running application. We might have demonstrated some mock transactions or models of the application at various times to them in the interim, but it wasn't the real application with real response times, throughput times, and actual transactions. So, again, there was usually some real disappointment at UAT with the application we had developed. In Agile, we're taking a very different approach. We're speeding up the feedback cycles with the customer in important ways, but also between all members of the project team.

The feedback cycles being used on an XP project are given in Figure 1.5.

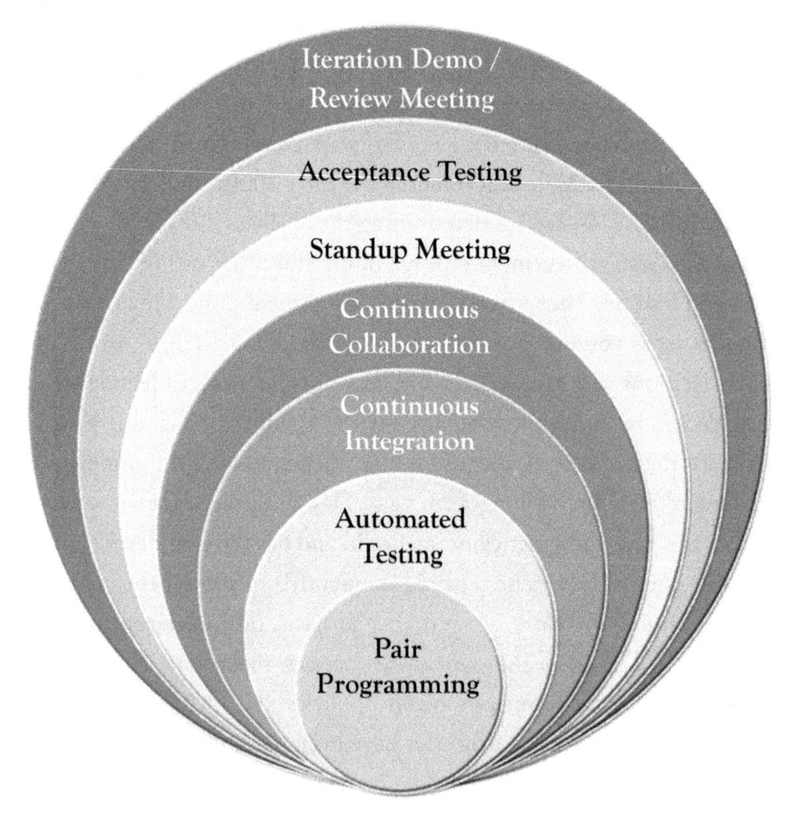

Figure 1.5 Levels of feedback and improvement and knowledge sharing—XP + Scrum

- Using "pair programming": code is tested in seconds.
- Unit test/automated testing: There is feedback in minutes.
- Continuous integration: Feedback in hours.
- Customer collaboration: Feedback in hours.
- Standup meeting: Feedback once a day.
- Acceptance test: Feedback in days.
- Iteration demo (review meeting): Feedback in weeks.
- Release review meeting: Feedback in months.

Increasing the frequency of communications with the customer and the feedback loops within the entire team significantly reduces the cost of change on a project. When I am teaching a PMP® Prep class, I get to a juncture in the class where I ask, "When do stakeholders have the most influence on a project?" And the students readily reply, "They will have the most influence, of course, at the very beginning of the project." And the reason is simple: the cost of change is the lowest at the beginning of the project. Once blueprints have been created for the project, then the stakeholders' influence has decreased, because if they change their mind on the design, they will have to throw out the existing blueprints and get new blueprints created. Of course, that is expensive. Once the actual construction of the building begins and a key stakeholder changes the design for the building, then the cost of change is prohibitively high. Their influence to change the project at that point is very limited; their influence decreases as the cost of change increases. So, we show the students a slide where we see the cost of change as a line running diagonally to the influence of stakeholders. It would look like that in Figure 1.6.

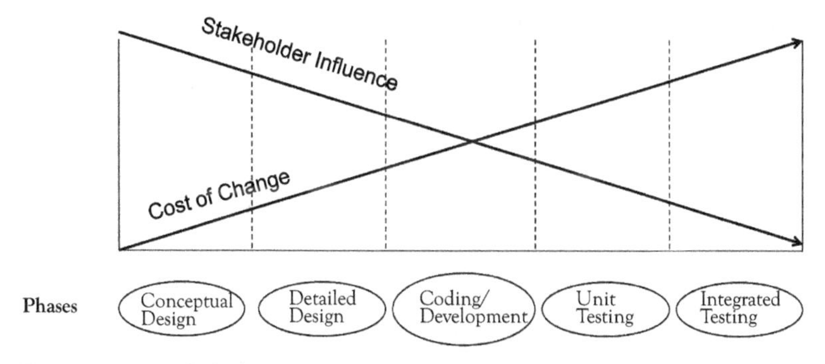

Figure 1.6 Stakeholder influence and cost of change in traditional projects

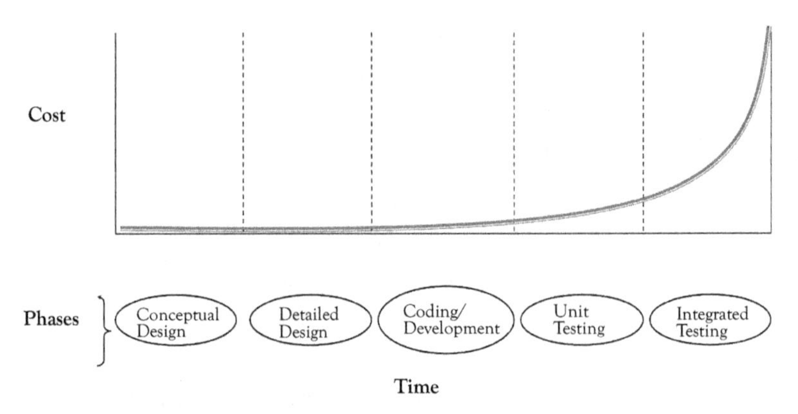

Figure 1.7 Real cost of change in traditional projects

However, for a project where we are creating a new software application or for a "knowledge work project," the cost of change line is not really a diagonal line. Since there is a lengthy period of time between the requirements gathering process and UAT—oftentimes more than a year—the cost of change line will have a nasty curve or uptick at the end of the project. Every change the customer wants at that point will have tremendous ramifications. Every change will touch many other parts of the project and will be very expensive. The cost of change line ends up looking like that in Figure 1.7.

With Agile approaches, by increasing the frequency of communications with the customer, by increasing the number and frequency of feedback loops, and by speeding up the PDCA loop, we flatten out the cost of change curve. Since we are meeting with the customer at minimum every month in iteration review meetings—but, in most cases much more frequently than that—the cost of change line looks like as in Figure 1.8.

Iteration 1	Iteration 2	Iteration 3	Iteration 4	Iteration 5
Sprint Planning Development Unit Testing Integrated Testing Sprint Review/Demo. Retrospective	Sprint Planning Development Unit Testing Integrated Testing Sprint Review/Demo. Retrospective	Sprint Planning Development Unit Testing Integrated Testing Sprint Rev./Demo Retrospective	Sprint Planning Development Unit Testing Integrated Testing Sprint Rev./Demo Retrospective	Sprint Planning Development Unit Testing Integrated Testing Sprint Review/Demo Retrospective

Cost

Figure 1.8 Reducing the "cost of change" with Agile

Jeff Sutherland gives us a couple of examples of how speeding up the feedback cycle and also the PDCA loop can reduce the cost on a project. These examples are provided in the section entitled "Do It Right the First Time" and "Fix Problems as Soon as You Find Them."[11] The first example involves a lesson learned at Palm in the early 2000s with their production of applications for personal digital assistants (PDAs). These devices were the predecessors of our smartphones today, and originally, they provided a number of applications such as a calendar function, spreadsheet software, and a notebook function. Palm learned that if a bug was discovered in a new application being developed, if the programmer fixed the bug immediately, it took one hour to make the fix. If the programmer waited three weeks, it took 24 hours to make the fix, or 24 times longer! A second example contrasts the way Toyota produces a Lexus today, with the way a Mercedes or BMW is built. A Lexus is made in 16.8 hours with 34 defects per 100 cars. If anyone on the team discovers a defect, they can stop production until the defect is fixed. In contrast, a BMW or Mercedes is made in 57 hours, and the German manufacturers do their quality testing after the car is produced. They spend more time fixing problems than Toyota does in producing their car!

Using Agile and Lean can provide tremendous advantages to us and help us avoid some of the classic pitfalls with our #1 Risk: a poorly written scope statement, or not being on the same page with the customer. This is especially important in our modern world of very volatile requirements and tremendous change: Tom Friedman's "world of accelerations." Also, providing something empirical and tangible to the product owner (and customer) on a very frequent basis has tremendous advantages. Again, Doug DeCarlo's quote is especially apt here, "If a picture is worth a thousand words, a prototype is worth a thousand pictures."

Sutherland says that the normal productivity gain from using Scrum will be 300 to 400 percent! Some teams have achieved an 800 percent improvement in productivity. He cites another case where a business friend was very impressed with a 25 to 35 percent improvement that they had achieved using Scrum. His immediate reaction was, "You must

[11] *Scrum: The Art of Doing Twice the Work in Half the Time* by Jeff Sutherland, J.J. Sutherland p. 97.

be doing something wrong!" The key benefit is not providing new tools for the development team. No, the key benefit is much more frequently demonstrating product increment to customers—the product owner—and determining what has value.

As we said, Lean is actually something that needs to be used all across the entire product lifecycle: from business development, through the project lifecycle, through testing, through QC and QA through integrating in Cybersecurity, and into the full part of the operational lifecycle. This is a key point the DevOps authors are making. In the *DevOps Handbook*, the authors say that after the manufacturing revolution of the 1980s, driven by Lean principles and practices and the Toyota Production System, "Organizations that did not implement lean practices lost market share, and many went out of business entirely."[12]

So, Agile and Lean are the solutions to all our problems, yes? (Silly rhetorical question, of course!) No, there is no one perfect process or solution to solving all our project management problems! There is no one process that's a panacea or which provides an easy way out. We have to be more flexible than that and realize we may have to use multiple processes and approaches. We're going to have to mix and match.

More than that, project management is hard work. That is just flat-out the case. Getting everyone onto the same page and prioritizing and getting agreement on requirements are hard work. We're negotiating, facilitating, communicating, and using all the soft-skill parts of project management to reach that goal. We're often working with very powerful stakeholders, who outrank us in our own organization or in outside organizations, and these stakeholders all have different needs, different wants, and different expectations for the project. This isn't going to be easy! There is a lot of pressure to meet very tight schedule constraints and budget constraints and achieve high quality. No pressure! The emphasis is clearly on the EQ part of the equation, not the IQ part of the equation.

Agile—by increasing the frequency of communications and by using "low tech and high touch" communications—is helping in key ways. But again, it's not a panacea.

---

[12] *The DevOps Handbook: How to Create World-Class Agility, Reliability and Security in Technology Organizations*— Gene Kim, Jez Humble, Patrick Debois, John Willis and John Allspaw—Location 515.

In the classic PMI® model (defined in the *PMBOK® Guide*) the PM is accountable for the project and for making all this happen. In the traditional or classic scenario, management wants that single point of contact for the project, or that "one throat to choke!" In the Agile model (especially with Scrum and XP) the closest role to the PM is the *Scrum Master* or the *Coach*. In Agile, the *Scrum Master* is not a "large and in-charge PM" or a traditional, fully accountable PM. The Scrum Master is a "servant leader" and his or her job is to make life easier for the team members.

Scrum Masters make sure other team members aren't interrupted and interfered with during the Sprint/Iteration. So, their job is "to carry food and carry water!" They are the owners of the methodology and the go-to person when there are questions about how to best use the methodology. However, the "team" all together (the developers, the Scrum Master, and the product owner) is accountable for the project! How can that possibly work? How can multiple people be accountable? Management is surely going to want that single point of contact. Yes? (That "one throat to choke!") Actually, this can work, and does work, because of the frequency of communications and the frequent feedback cycles. The idea is that management (and also the product owner) can wait one to four weeks for the end of the Sprint/Iteration for the review meeting to inspect the product increment (deliverable that was created in the Sprint), decide if this deliverable(s) meets the "definition of done," and decide whether it is acceptable. The entire team is accountable for what has been created in the iteration and what is being demonstrated in the review meeting.

Problem Areas for Agile

Agile is not a perfect solution for all projects. What are some key problem areas and some key types of projects where Agile is not a good fit, and why? Here are a few examples to use as a starting point for our next section on "How Do We Make Hybrid Approaches Work?"

1. If we do not have the right type of working relationship with our key stakeholders—the sponsor and other senior managers, customer, functional managers, and other stakeholders—then Agile is not going to work as it should. As was said before, it is best to use Agile for projects when the customer doesn't know exactly what they

want starting out in the project, and we need to discover and explore requirements. Thus, there is a premium being put on creativity. Therefore, the team needs to be provided a lot of freedom and trust in exploring what the best solution might be. It follows that Agile is not going to be the best fit in the following circumstances:

- If there is a lack of trust or working experience with all the stakeholders and stakeholder groups.
- If the customer and management do not accept that we are in a "time and materials world" where we need to discover and explore requirements, then Agile is not going to be the best fit. Management must understand the benefits of Lean and Agile and must understand they need to be involved in the review meetings and the frequent feedback loops for this to work. If they are insisting on fixed schedule constraints where fixed detailed design objectives must be met, this is not the right fit.[13]
- If management thinks Agile is just a nice set of tools for the developers and programmers that will increase their produc-

[13] The acceptance criteria, or "definition of done," will be more high level (as in a Dynamic Systems Development Method, DSDM, contract type) than they would be in a fixed-price (FFP) contract. They will be about high-level functional requirements, not detailed engineering design requirements. A number of different engineering designs could meet the functional, high-level requirements, and we are entrusting the team to explore and discover the right engineering design. So, management must be accepting of this. There must be more flexibility, trust, and tolerance in assessing what meets the definition of done. But we are more in the world of IKIWISI—"I'll know it when I see it!" So, management must understand this well. We can't start out the project with preconceived notions and demands for the final detailed engineering design. Also, we can't have the situation where we sell the concept of Agile and Lean to management; at the outset of the project they profess to be quite accepting of this approach, and say they see the benefits; then, in the middle of the project, "life happens!" Some emergency comes up, and management quickly reverts back to a classic mindset and insists on fixed constraints for time and cost, but also fixed scope requirements that are detailed engineering requirements. This was not the agreement between management and the team starting out. We must have a strong relationship between management and team and know there won't be such a change in mindset partway into the project.

tivity and they do not have to get involved, then this is not going to work. Using Agile will not meet expectations.

- If management doesn't provide the right culture for the Agile team members, a "Theory Y type environment,"[14] empowering the team and providing a lot of freedom and trust, then this is not going to work well.[15] We will explore this topic in more depth in the section "How Do We Make Hybrid Approaches Work?"

---

[14] "Theory X" companies and "Theory X" managers start with the belief that their employees do not enjoy their job and do not enjoy work. If you start with that premise, then you will believe your employees will be lazy, careless, inefficient, and unmotivated. You will have to micromanage them closely to achieve the right business results. "Theory Y" companies and managers start with the opposite belief. They believe their employees do enjoy work, want to do a good job, and if they are provided freedom and trust, they will achieve the right business results.

[15] Many Agilists think they invented this enlightened culture of providing freedom and trust to the team members (the "Agile Ethos"). They did not! I believe this culture really started with Hewlett-Packard in 1939 and was a core part of the "HP Way." This became the foundation of most companies in Silicon Valley from the mid-1970s through the early 1990s. Walter Isaacson, in his book, *The Innovators: How a Group of Hackers, Geniuses, and Geeks Created the Digital Revolution,* describes very well how this culture originated in HP in the early 1940s, and later spread through other Tech companies such as Intel in Silicon Valley. Bill Hewlett, in defining the HP Way, said, "We believe people want to do a good job, and we're going to provide them that opportunity. We are going to provide them the right environment, but then trust that they will achieve the right business goals." … "We believe the people closest to the problem will have the best solution. We will not micromanage them. We will define the high-level strategic goals, but empower people closest to the problem to come up with the right solution." . . . "We also believe that people are our most valuable resource." … "If we succeed as a company, our people should succeed." They backed this up with a very enlightened profit-sharing program and employee stock program at a time when this was almost unheard of. It breaks my heart that in the early 2000s with new management, very large mergers and acquisitions, much of this amazing culture began to be dismantled. Other Silicon Valley companies also seemed to depart from this enlightened model, but the most successful Tech companies of the past 10 to 15 years, Google and Apple, have kept this culture alive and well. I think keeping this culture alive was a big part of their success!

- If we are subcontracting much of the project work to vendors, and we have very little past-performance information for these vendors, then Agile is not a good fit. We will need a detailed SOW with all the I's dotted and T's crossed.

2. Large, complex projects with many stakeholders and stakeholder groups—difficulty finding the right product owner who can resolve conflicts.
   - Jeff Sutherland describes several projects[16] (the FBI Sentinel Project, Medco, etc.), which were all in crisis and failing, but in all these projects there were a large number of stakeholders and stakeholder groups that had disparate needs and wants that were not compatible, and the projects were stuck in a deadlocked position. The stakeholders were at loggerheads about what should be included in the project and what the priorities should be. One of the first goals in transitioning to Scrum is to simplify this type of situation. For the FBI Sentinel project, they reduced the staff from 220 to 40 and reduced the number of FBI employees on the project from 30 to 12. The next step focused on prioritizing the requirements—or the product backlog—and identifying the 20 percent of the requirements that would achieve 80 percent of the need. Having the right product owner, if that can be achieved, will definitely help resolve deadlocks in choosing what should be included in the product backlog and the priorities of these backlog items. But, on some very large complex projects, it may be necessary to have multiple product owners and, of course, that can present problems too. Someone has to have the final say and be the decision maker. And, if the right product owner is not selected, and if senior management ends up vetoing what the product owner had previously approved, but only after three or more months have passed, then we will have wasted a tremendous amount

[16] *Scrum: The Art of Doing Twice the Work in Half the Time* by Jeff Sutherland, J.J. Sutherland.

of time and a lot of money, and Agile didn't work the way it was intended.

- So, it might be difficult to find the right product owner (or "Customer" in XP). A key assumption for Scrum (or for XP) is that we can find the right product owner, who will effectively resolve the conflicts between incompatible requirements for what will be included in the project and define priorities. But, on a large, complex project with many powerful stakeholders, it may be very difficult to get agreement and get all the stakeholders to buy into what the product owner has decided. Again, as we described earlier, this is the hard part of project management! Whether it is a PM or a product owner striving to get agreement on inconsistent, incompatible requirements, this can be a very tough challenge to handle. Many large, complex projects and programs (F-22, Affordable Care Act website, etc.) have failed because this wasn't handled correctly. No matter what powers have been given to the product owner, there will be many other stakeholders on the project (e.g., the sponsor, the customer, other senior managers, federal regulatory agencies) that outrank the product owner. The skillsets the product owner must employ to get everyone onto the same page are "soft skills": negotiation skills, communication skills, facilitation skills, and so on. Following a particular process, or even a methodology, will not guarantee success in achieving this goal. This is about the "EQ" part of the equation, not the "IQ" part!

3. We are in a "cookie-cutter" type project and have successfully done very similar projects like this one many times before. There were only small customizations differentiating the projects. (Again, does that mean this type of project is easy? No!) However, if we are in a "cookie-cutter" type project, it will be far less expensive and more efficient and practical to use the traditional approach.
   - We don't need to discover and explore requirements: The customer knows going in exactly what they want for this project. We need a traditional SOW where all the "I's are dotted, and T's are crossed!" (e.g., A young couple is remod-

eling their kitchen, and the key stakeholder—the wife, of course!—knows exactly what she wants going in—the make and models for the different appliances, the exact type of cabinets and countertops, etc.)

4. We are handling an emergency situation, and there isn't time to explore or discover requirements: There isn't time to prototype. (There might not be time to canvass all the stakeholders and exhaustively detail all the requirements either!) We may be in the type of situation where "A less than optimal decision made now—at the right time—is better than the perfect decision made too late."
5. We have only one chance to do this project, and we have to get things right the first time (e.g., again, perhaps an emergency rescue mission: Apollo 13!).
6. Places where more central control is needed. (The classic PMP®—fully accountable PM is needed.) Perhaps this could be for an emergency situation or a military operation. There isn't time to debate different solutions; we need the team members to follow through on the plans being disseminated by the PM.
7. If the team members are multitasking on a number of projects at the same time, are only able to perform very specialized tasks within their range of expertise, and are only working part-time on the project, then Agile probably isn't the best fit.
8. If the team cannot come up with an "MVP" (minimum viable product) to demonstrate to the product owner and customer in the early iterations, Agile is probably not a good fit. For a large, complex project, it might take a development team many months to tie together all of the infrastructure and hardware before any kind of recognizable demo or MVP can be made. In the early iterations, it might only be possible to demonstrate something using prototypes or models with "fake data." Engineers and customers could sit side-by-side with the product owner and customer, discuss the prototype, and talk abstractly about what features the customer would like the real product to have or how they would like to use it. But then there will often be a large effort and a long period of time to get a real working product created that is usable by customers. These "planning phases" of the project could take months, and a predictive

planning approach will probably be needed. In this situation, we cannot effectively use Lean and Agile. We are relegated to using a traditional, predictive planning approach. When you have an MVP or demo that uses real customer data, that is the type of project where you can meet with the customer in the first iterations and effectively use Lean and Agile.[17]

Other Key Risks Where Agile Provides Extra Help

It's a well-known maxim that when projects fail, they fail at the very beginning. We said that having a poorly written scope statement (which stemmed from not doing requirements well) was the #1 cause of project failure and was, therefore, our #1 Risk! As we said, this often stems from not doing requirements well and "not being on the same page" with the customer and senior management. This is certainly something that hits many projects right at the very beginning. We saw how using Lean and Agile methodologies can help us handle this risk. By going after the top priority requirements first (20 percent of the requirements that will fulfill 80 percent of the business need in the first iterations of the project), we are addressing this risk. By increasing the frequency of the feedback loops and speeding up the PDCA loop, we are addressing this risk. There are three more key risks that also occur right at the beginning of projects that Agile can help us solve:

1. Allowing half-baked ideas to survive and not doing "kill points" well
2. Handling "impossible constraints" or dealing with the "impossible project"
3. Poor communications: not keeping senior management in the loop and up-to-date on the project[18]

---

[17] I would like to thank Jason Vorenkamp for providing this important example! Jason said it was fairly common to run into this issue with a number of IT projects where they were using Agile.

[18] Again, I'm being a little bit lazy in describing these three items all as "risks!" If any of the items involve uncertainty and are something that could happen in the future, then they are risks. If the problems have already occurred, they are no longer risks; they are "issues." Agile will help us in handling these, no matter whether they still are risks or are issues.

Risk #2: Allowing Half-Baked Ideas to Survive

If we are worth our salt at all as PMs, we are focusing very heavily on managing risk. We are doing this at the very start of the project and also all throughout the project. Risk Management must be focused on, iteratively, throughout the project. If we don't do this, there is no way to be proactive and no way to issue the favorite type of change request for PMI®—"Preventive Change Requests." If our team members are not on the lookout for triggers of negative risks, then there is no way we will be able to put into action strategies for avoiding these negative risks, mitigating negative risks, or transferring negative risks. So, doing Risk Management is absolutely fundamental and necessary on all projects.

We are also focusing on risks in a number of different categories and we are using a risk breakdown structure (RBS) to help us identify risks in these categories. Early on in my career as a PM, I used an RBS that started with risks at the top and then, in the next level down, I broke risks into "internal risks" and "external risks." So, we can make that type of structure work fine, but what I prefer, today, is the RBS (Figure 1.9) Doug DeCarlo uses in his book *Extreme Project Management.*

The second level in DeCarlo's RBS is divided between (1) "business risks," (2) "product risks" or "technical risks," (3) "project risks," and last (4) "organizational risks."

Business risks are all about the risks of profit and loss: what senior managers and our sponsor are most focused on! Is the idea of this project totally half-baked? Are we going to make a profit, or are we going to lose our shirt? Is this something that we are good at? How is the economy? Is this a very tough competitive landscape? Is this a highly regulated marketplace? We are focusing on those types of questions. Too many times, companies go after a totally half-baked idea or some senior manager's pet project or something that we are really clueless about. This is a very dangerous situation. If management allows such half-baked ideas to survive, then very valuable resources and funding are being taken from other much more deserving projects. This can even lead to the downfall of the entire company! So, we need to find out about the validity of a project idea very early on in the game and kill the project if it is a half-baked idea.

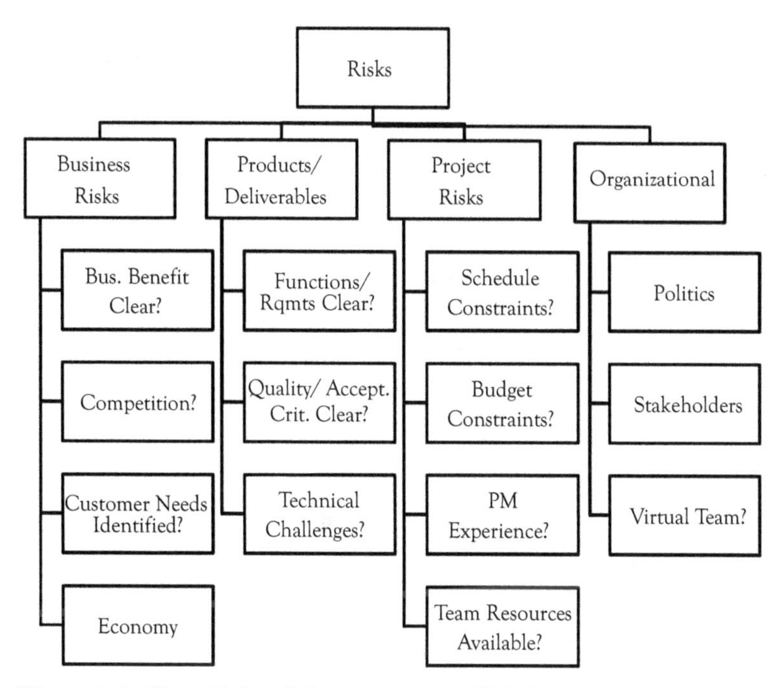

Figure 1.9 The risk breakdown structure (RBS)

By the way, if we are asked to manage a project that is totally half-baked, is this mostly a risk just for senior management and the sponsor or is this a big risk for us, too? Again, an obviously rhetorical question! Of course, this is a huge risk for us as PMs. This project is certainly bound to fail, and when it fails, who is going to take the blame? Who is going to be looking for a new job? You know the answer, and it's not the sponsor who came up with the half-baked idea.

Before I move on to talk more about business risks and half-baked ideas, let's talk briefly about the other three major categories of risk in this RBS. The second category—product risks or technical risks—is focusing on questions such as "Do we have the resources and skill sets to create the product with the right quality?" Are the requirements and the quality metrics for these products clearly defined and specified; are they SMART? The third category—project risks—is primarily focusing on constraints. How tightly constrained is this project? Are there very tough budget constraints, schedule constraints, or resource constraints? Have we correctly identified the priorities of the triple constraints? Also, do we have the right PM with the right experience? The last category—organizational risks—is all about political risk. We are creating something new and unique. Yes? That is what a project is all about: creating either a new product, a new service, or a result. That's the definition of a project in the *PMBOK® Guide.*

So, is everyone in our organization in favor of this project, this new thing we are trying to create? Of course not! Some people are losing power and influence because of our project. They are not in favor of this project at all. Many people resist change and just don't understand change. They are saying things like, "What was wrong with the way we used to do things?" or "I like the old way!" They are not in favor of this project, either. So, when we created our *Stakeholder Management* strategies, we should have focused on these stakeholders and tried to put together strategies to turn the more negative stakeholders into supporters of the project, or at least neutralize the negativity.

Back to "half-baked ideas"—"kill points" and handling business risks ...

When I obtained my PMP® certification in 1995, the requirements for contact hours, or education hours, were more stringent for the PMP® certification. Therefore, HP sent me to a two-day conference on project management held at Boston University, so I could obtain the necessary contact hours. There were more than 25 different presentations delivered (some simultaneously in different rooms) over the two days, and prizes were awarded for the best papers. The first prize went to *Ten Dumb Mistakes That Project Managers Make* by Gopal Kapur. The number one mistake that he listed was "Allowing half-baked ideas to survive."

Classically, when product managers and the business development team are working with senior managers to do project selection, they are using financial selection techniques such as net present value (NPV), internal rate of return (IRR), opportunity costs, pay-back period, economic value add (EVA), and other methods to see what project will have the greatest return on investment (ROI). Mr. Kapur's point was that all too often, these techniques are only used once to select a project out of a possible group of projects, and then management never reanalyzes things or re-examines things to determine if the business case still exists for the project. His point was that this should be done multiple times through the course of the project lifecycle. (Perhaps this should be done at the end of every phase to see if we think we will still get the best ROI with the project.)

As we move through every step of planning, we are progressively elaborating and decomposing high-level business requirements and functional requirements down to more detailed products, and more detailed products down to parts and components, and parts and components down to specific activities. Therefore, we can obtain much better estimates of time and cost each step of the way and also improve our forecasts for the project. These better estimates and forecasts should be fed back into the financial analysis techniques, so we can determine if the business case still exists. Many companies do not do this at all or do not do it well, and this can lead to immense problems. We want to ensure that we aren't attempting to create something "half-baked" that has very little chance of being on-time, within budget, and having the desired value for our customer.

In Figure 1.10, we are showing kill points occurring regularly as we move through the project phases.

Agile is helping the product owner, senior management, and the team accomplish the "kill points" in a much more effective way. First, the kill points can occur much earlier and much more frequently. Review meetings with the product owner and management are occurring at minimum on a monthly basis, but oftentimes are occurring much more frequently than that. Management and other stakeholders are encouraged to come by the area where the team is working on a frequent basis to review the "information radiator" that displays the burndown chart, a Kanban Board, and other key information on the project's progress, so they can discuss the project and ask questions.

More than that, something empirical and tangible is being produced in each iteration, and as we've said this is much more valuable than only producing dashboard reports displaying S-curves, network diagrams, Gantt charts, or other forecasts. When we're in the type of project where the customer doesn't know exactly what they want going into the project and we need to explore and discover the best solution, providing something empirical that the product owner can touch, experiment with, and use will be especially valuable. Again, we could be in the world of "I'll know it when I see it"—or IKIWISI!

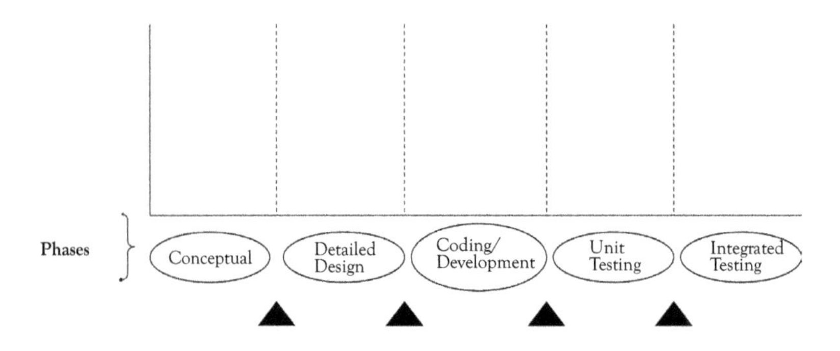

Figure 1.10 Project lifecycle (divide the project into phases)

Risk #3: Impossible Constraints

A type of risk closely related to the problem of a project dealing with a "half-baked idea" is the problem of dealing with the "impossible project." I think all PMs have been put in the situation where the sales team has thrown a new project over the fence to them with an impossible schedule constraint; or similarly, senior management imposes upon them an impossible budget constraint for a project. (These risks fit into the category of "project risk" in our earlier RBS.) Unfortunately, all too often, the sales people and the management team did not bring the PM into the presales process fully and did not ask for the PM's opinion early on for figuring out what was realistic for the project and what could be achieved. In today's world where the competitive bar has been set very high, customers are more fickle than ever, and the marketplace is changing so fast it makes your head spin. This scenario is far too common! PMs are being asked to manage the "impossible project!"

The PM is left wondering, "What were they thinking, and how in the heck did they expect that this project could get done?" "I wish they would come and try managing this project!" When the senior manager asks the PM, "Now, you can get this project successfully completed. Yes?" "You can get this project completed on time and within budget. Yes?" What's the right answer? Is it, "Sir, yes Sir!" "I know you have given us a very challenging schedule here, and of course, not all the resources we would like to have, but I am very confident in our team, and I know the team and I will be successful in meeting your goals!" And then, "At this moment, I'm not quite sure how we will pull this off, but with hard work, I know we can succeed, and we will succeed!" Is this the right answer? Of course not! Management does not need some Pollyanna, glib answer; they do not need a yes-man to tell them what they want to hear. That isn't going to do them any good at all. They do need some type of reality check and good advice on what can realistically be expected with the project. So, what is the right answer? (And this answer applies to either the traditional waterfall model or the Agile model.) The answer is, "I don't know yet!" "We need to do some more planning and investigation to determine what can be accomplished, and in what time frames, and for what cost." "The team and I will do this more detailed planning, but I will get back to you soon with much better estimates of time and cost for what we are confident we can accomplish."

What would our approach be using a traditional waterfall project lifecycle? As we said before, we would just follow the sequence of planning processes that are laid out in the first Knowledge Areas in the *PMBOK® Guide*. As we've already described, we would take the initial description of what product or service best meets the business need from the project charter, plus the initial estimates of time, cost, resources, and risk, and we would start drilling into more detail. We would do the process, *Collect Requirements*, very well, ensuring that we did not miss any requirements, misunderstand any requirements, or miss any stakeholders. We would then do the process, *Define Scope*, and define boundaries and exclusions for our deliverables and make sure that everyone is on the same page for this project. However, we wouldn't stop there. We would keep going deeper into what PMI® loves best: *Create WBS*. Then, we would go down to the activity level with our scheduling processes. All along, we've been improving time estimates and cost estimates for budgeting. Each step of the way through planning, we are drilling into more and more detail: we break down high-level requirements into specific deliverables, then down to parts and then to components of parts; we will know resources much better, so we can provide much better estimates of time and cost. On a large, complex project, how long is this going to take? Probably several months at minimum!

Is management going to be patient with us over these months, waiting to get the better estimates of time and cost? Of course not! They are knocking on our door every few days demanding these better estimates. We are doing our best to oblige, using estimating techniques described in the *PMBOK® Guide—Analogous Estimating, Bottom-Up Estimating, Parametric Estimating, and Three-Point Estimating.* As we move through the sequence of these planning processes described above, we are understanding our products and deliverables in more detail each step of the way, breaking things down to the part level, component level, and then the activity level, so each step of the way we can obtain more accurate estimates of time and cost. In addition, we will use the analytic techniques described in the process, *Perform Quantitative Risk Analysis*, by first obtaining probability distributions for time and cost for work-packages or even the activities in the schedule, and then using Monte Carlo simulation to mathematically determine the right level of contingency reserves that should be included with activities that will roll up to the schedule baseline and the cost baseline to help protect the project from risk. Therefore, we will be able to get a more accurate forecast of when this project is likely to finish and a more accurate budget forecast. Alternatively, we may choose to use EMV to refine the contingency reserves.

Using these estimating methods and other analytic tools and techniques, we will have created a very impressive network diagram showing the dependencies between the thousands of activities in the project, the critical path for the project, and the float for all the activities in the network diagram. Using Monte Carlo, we could create a very impressive S-curve[19] showing a probability distribution of projected costs for the project, and then we could explain to management what this implies for our level of confidence of meeting certain schedule objectives and cost objectives. We could create a tornado diagram that shows what work-packages are most sensitive to what risks. Doing all this planning and creating all these charts that took months and months can be very seductive, and create some very impressive charts and documents. But, how accurate and how reliable will all these charts be? How accurate will our forecasts be? In our modern project world, with so much change and volatility, it is very rare that these will be accurate. As Jeff Sutherland describes in his book on Scrum,

---

[19] See Figure 1.11 which provides an example of an S-curve. An explanation of an S-curve is also provided.

It's just so tempting to draw up endless charts. All the work needed to be done on a massive project laid out for everyone to see—but when detailed plans meet reality, they fall apart. Build into your working method the assumption of change, discovery, and new ideas.

Several other excellent quotes also bear on this subject:

- "To fail to plan is to plan to fail." Yes, very true, but also…
- "Planning is useful. Blindly following plans is stupid!"
- "Planning for combat is important, but as soon as the first shot is fired, your plans go up in smoke."—Dwight Eisenhower
- "No plan survives contact with the enemy."—Helmuth von Moltke the Elder (Prussian General)

In an interesting book, *The Six Dimensions of Project Management: Turning Constraints into Resources* by Michael Dobson and Heidi Feickert, the authors describe how we can sometimes solve the "impossible project" by figuring out which of our triple constraints has the highest priority, which is second in priority, and which is third, and then, using creativity and one's imagination and by being proactive, we might be able to exploit one of these constraints or project assumptions. They point out examples of situations where it was assumed something was a fixed constraint, but by being proactive, using creativity, and thinking "out of the box," it was discovered there were assumptions buried in the constraint, and using creativity, the assumptions could be changed and the supposed constraint could also be changed. The constraints weren't really constraints after all! This should be reminiscent of the Standish survey, and the point made previously about requirements: "65 percent of the requirements the customer thinks are absolutely necessary will never be used!" In our projects, it often turns out that requirements that were thought to be absolutely necessary are found not to be needed.

Therefore, Agile methodologies will provide a much more effective and faster solution for probing what is really an assumption and what is a constraint.[20] By going after the highest priority requirements in our first iterations (the 20 percent of the requirements that will fulfill 80 percent of the need) and also the requirements with the most risk, and then by creating something tangible and empirical that can be demonstrated to the product owner (and the customer and other senior managers), we should be able to solve problems with impossible constraints much more effectively. We will see very early in the project what has value and what does not. Things that don't have value will be taken out of the product backlog, and we will not invest in them further. As we said before, this is going to save time and money. Demonstrating something tangible and empirical to our key stakeholders also provides a much stronger reality check on the value of what's being created. (Doug DeCarlo's quote: "If a picture is worth a thousand words, a prototype is worth a thousand pictures!") As we saw in the Medco example earlier, using Scrum, or another Agile methodology, and using Lean approaches can solve the problem with handling an impossible constraint. Even if we find out that what we are trying to achieve is truly impossible, and this cannot be accomplished in the right time frame for the right budget, and meet mandatory scope and quality requirements, then at least we have determined that very early in the project, in the first iterations. We can provide the product owner and senior management the information they need to make an informed decision on whether or not they should cancel this project. That may be the best thing to do in a number of cases. The project team may be very discouraged with this outcome, but it might be the best choice for the company. Increasing the frequency of the feedback loops and speeding up

[20] By the way, the pure definition of a constraint for PMI® is "Constraints are things that are given to us from the outside, and limit our options for planning." These are things that are known or are facts. There are six classic constraints: scope, time, cost, resources, risk, and quality. Or... We can have constraints in any of the six areas. For PMI®, in contrast, assumptions are things that we assume to be true for the time being that will guide planning. At the beginning of my project, I often make assumptions about resources, and what training is required for my resources, or what tools and equipment will be required for my resources. I may assume going into the project that my resources won't need more training or won't need new software or new tools. We always need to re-examine our assumptions as we are moving through the project.

the PDCA loop also help management in making better decisions with the kill points. As we said previously, many companies don't do these "kill points" very well, and this can lead to huge problems.

Even while using traditional project management approaches, the importance of getting off to a good start is well known. In the literature, it's well understood that the number one risk we face is not getting off to a good start, not obtaining requirements in the right way, and not having a well-written scope statement with boundaries and exclusions and SMART acceptance criteria for our deliverables.

EVM which, as we've said, is very consistent with traditional waterfall project management also understands this very well. In Fleming and Koppelman's book, *Simple Earned Value on All Projects (Simplified Translations of the 27 EVM Criteria)*, they point out that it's most important to use EV, get the key measurements of schedule variance (SV), cost variance (CV), cost performance index (CPI), and schedule performance index (SPI), and also get our forecasts, estimate at completion (EAC), and estimate to completion (ETC) very early in the project lifecycle. We really need to get these EV measurements no later than 15 to 20 percent into the project schedule.[21] It's only at that point where we have some hope of making the necessary corrections to save the project! If we are more than one-third of the way through the project, and we discover that CPI is significantly below one (e.g., 0.8), then it's too late to make the corrections. To-complete performance index (TCPI) will be some number like 1.2, which is saying we need to make a 40 percent improvement in our budget performance to get back to the original budget, the original BAC. That is not possible, and there is a "small chance out of no chance" of that happening! They point out that there is a wealth of data on federal programs—many of them large DoD programs—where it is shown that once you're more than 15 percent through the project schedule, it's next

---

[21] "Using data from a sample of completed Air Force contracts, Christensen/Payne establish that the cumulative CPI did not change by more than 10% from the value at the 20% contract completion point. Based on data from the Defense acquisition executive summary (DAE S) database, results indicate that the cumulative CPI is stable from the 20% completion point regardless of contract type, program, or service." p. 41.

to impossible to make more than a 5 or 8 percent improvement in CPI or the budget performance. So, to be useful for us, EVM must be used very early on in the project lifecycle.

Agile methodologies are providing the same type of performance measurements very early in the project lifecycle, even in our first iterations, using burndown charts and burnup charts. These are much more intuitive and easier to understand than the EVM dashboard, which is typically an S-curve showing all the EVM variables—planned value (PV), earned value (EV), actual cost (AC), Budget at Completion (BAC)—and also showing forecasts—estimate at completion (EAC) and estimate to completion (ETC). There are few senior managers who will understand the intricacies of such an S-curve, but almost anyone is quickly going to grasp what a burndown chart is indicating and will be able to make the appropriate inferences to see when we're going to end up with this project.

A Classic S-Curve Chart

A classic S-curve chart[22] is given in Figure 1.11 and a classic burndown chart in Figure 1.12.

The dashed line on the burndown chart is showing us our plan for creating work or creating story points. Thus, the descending dashed line is showing us the remaining PV in the project or in the release. The solid line is showing us the work we've actually created, or story points actually created, so this is showing us EV (actually, the remaining EV as the line descends). AC is also easy to derive as the costs for each iteration are fixed, since these are essentially the labor costs for each iteration. Though we

[22] In EVM, the cost baseline is usually represented as an S-Curve: a time-phased budget or a curve showing the cumulative spend-rate for the project. In a classic waterfall project, the costs start out low in the early phases of a project. (We have fewer people working on the project in the early planning phases, and a lower use of tools and equipment.) During the "execution phase(s)," costs start accelerating, and typically, in the middle of the execution phases, the project experiences its highest spend-rate. Then as work is completed, the resources doing the work can be released, so the spend-rate for the project begins to decline. This "time-phased" budget or cost baseline is an "S" lying on its side. In EVM, this is called the "performance measurement baseline."

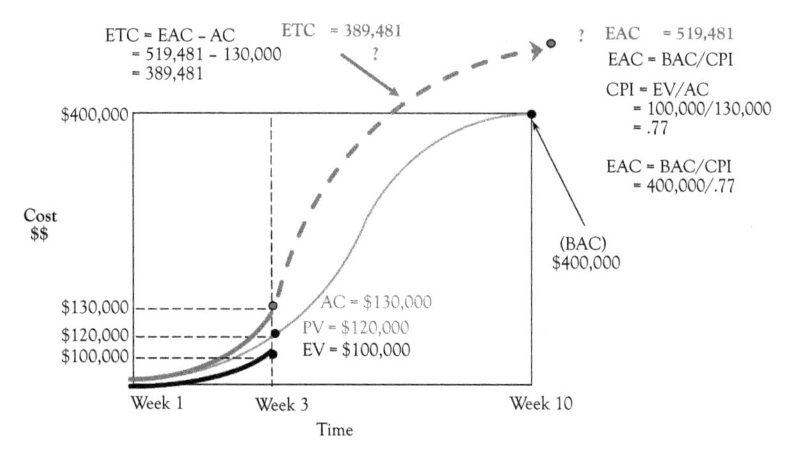

Figure 1.11 Cost baseline = a classic "S-curve"

didn't show it, this would be a diagonal line running from the bottom left to the upper right (the opposite direction of the dashed line). To stay consistent with the theme of the burndown chart, we could make the AC line a descending line that is showing us costs remaining in the project. Again, the costs should be fixed for the project or the release.

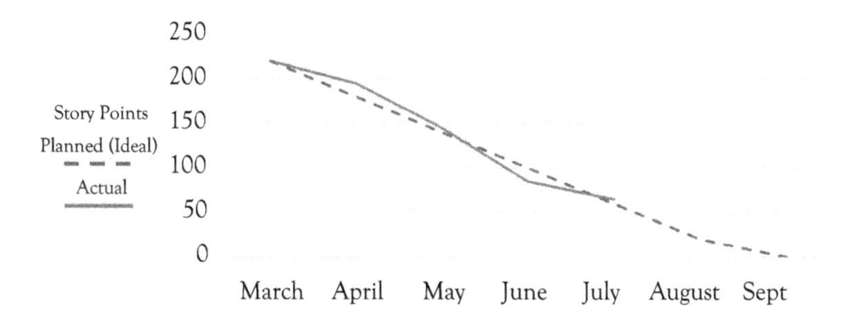

Figure 1.12 Burndown chart

Risk #4: Poor Communications: Not Keeping Senior Management in the Loop and Up-to-Date on the Project

As PMs, we all know how important it is to do communications very well on our projects. Our most important skillset as a PM is communications skills. As we've said, a huge part of this is good listening skills: "All good communicators are necessarily good listeners." A big part of good communications and good listening skills is paying close attention to all the "undercurrents" involved in the communications—all the body language. Again, I think 90 percent of good project management is really about emotional intelligence—the "EQ part of the equation," not the technical part or the "IQ part of the equation." For almost every project I've encountered that was failing and in crisis, there were serious communications problems.

What does senior management—and the customer, too—hate most? Surprises! Negative surprises! But not keeping them up-to-date on the progress and the good things happening with our project is also a dangerous mistake, especially not updating our sponsor. If we have not kept her in the loop on progress being made and our success, then "out of sight is out of mind." Other priorities might have come up, and she might have shifted her focus elsewhere. We might find she has decided to shift resources or funding from our project to something new.

On a critical project I managed at HP—one of those "impossible projects"—in our internal kickoff meeting, the sponsor said to the team, "It will not be enough to just communicate well on this project, we must 'over-communicate!'" So, what did he mean? This project was a special project with an incredibly demanding go-live date, $80 million plus at stake, a very difficult external customer to keep happy, a very large number of key stakeholders, other business units inside of HP,—and also key vendors to whom we had subcontracted major portions of the project.

How many times in your project do you believe you have done all the necessary things to get agreement between key stakeholders on an important date, or a requirement, or item, or decision, and things still went wrong? You ensured minutes were taken of the meeting where the agreement was achieved, and the minutes documented that everyone agreed with several key decisions. The minutes were disseminated properly to all the key parties soon after the meeting, and yet, somehow, things still did not go smoothly. You asked all the attendees of the meeting to review the minutes and report back by the end of the next day with any corrections or edits. Then, a few weeks later, a key stakeholder says, "No, I didn't say that." ... or ... "That is not exactly what I meant." Sometimes, when we get the answer, "Yes," on a key point, we need to double-check with that stakeholder a few days later, and make sure the answer is still yes! I believe this is what the sponsor meant by saying, "We must over-communicate." This is probably not necessary on all projects, but at some time in your career as a PM, it will be!

In Gopal Kapur's presentation, *Ten Dumb Mistakes Project Managers Make*, the number one mistake was allowing "half-baked ideas to survive." The number two mistake was not keeping your sponsor and other key stakeholders in the loop with key status information on the project. He termed this, "Overlooking stakeholders, forgetting the champions, and ignoring the nemesis."

We have already seen how Agile really helps in key ways with improving communications for our project. We've described that with using Agile:

1. We are communicating with the product owner, customer, and other key stakeholders much more frequently.
    - Review meetings are occurring, at minimum, on a monthly basis, but collaboration with the key stakeholders is expected to be occurring more frequently than that.
2. Communications between all team members are occurring much more frequently.
    - Daily standup meetings with the team members are an excellent tool for improving communications. Every team member gets to hear how things are going with all the other team members, what problems they're facing, and what progress they're making. When they hear of a problem another team member is having, it is likely that one of the team members is going to have some suggestions. This is taken off-line, and not handled in the standup meeting, but this will very likely help improve progress for the project.

- Retrospective meetings that are held at minimum in each iteration are also excellent tools for improving communications and improving the team chemistry. At heart, these are just "lessons learned meetings." These retrospective meetings are for the team members and ways for them to improve their processes: At the end of each Sprint (Iteration), they are asking, "What worked well?" ... "What didn't work so well?" ... "What should we do differently in the next Sprint?"
- The frequency of the "feedback loops" is dramatically increased. Agile is speeding up the PDCA loop, and this is speeding up communications.

3. We are demonstrating tangible, empirical "product increment" to the stakeholders. This is more compelling and powerful than just reporting our project dashboard in "S-curves," progress reports, status reports, forecasts, or other EVM reports.
4. The Agile reports—"the information radiator"—is "low tech" and "high touch." These reports such as a burndown chart, burnup chart, Kanban Board, and reports showing the team's velocity are intuitive and easily understood. It's a very rare customer or senior manager who understands all the vagaries and details in an EVM S-curve. On the other hand, they will readily understand a burndown chart, Kanban Board, or report showing velocity.
5. What management cares most about are our forecasts. They do care about our variances, our CPI, and where we are today with the project, but the question most on their mind is, "When will you really be done?" ... and of course, "How much is this project really going to cost when it's all said and done?" That is the reason *Cost Forecasts* are the most important output of *Control Costs*, and *Schedule Forecasts* are the most important output of *Control Schedule* in the *PMBOK® Guide*. It is far easier to forecast using a burndown chart or burnup chart, than to do forecasting with Monte Carlo or EVM.
6. Using dedicated teams that are colocated will improve communications in very significant ways. If the team is colocated, what did we just get rid of? Phone tag! Delays and waiting for responses to email messages! Also, how many times have you received an email from a

> key stakeholder where you thought everything was under control and you were on the same page, together, regarding the project. You read this email, and it's obvious that you're not on the same page. You are reading the email, and parts of it are very confusing and obscure. You're wondering why they said things the way that they did, and you know there's some type of problem, but you're not really sure what that problem is.

In the world in which I managed projects, it's very unlikely that I'm in the same office with this stakeholder. I'm going to have to pick up the phone and, hopefully, get them on the phone right away, and try to get to the bottom of this problem. But, more times than not, I'll reach their voicemail, and I'll have to leave a message. Then, I'll be quite frustrated—for at least several hours until we can get to the bottom of things. If I'm in an Agile environment where the entire team is colocated, I can just get up out of my chair, go find this stakeholder, and we will quickly get to the bottom of things. What's the key factor that's really going to help me cut through any possible confusion and nonsense? Being able to see the body language of this other stakeholder is key. Being able to see their expressions and hear the tone of their voice will be vital in ensuring that we are on the same page. In a classic Agile environment, I can get all of that. As Susan Parente discusses in the chapter on "Virtual Agile Teams," we will need good tools like Zoom, GoToMeeting, Google Hangouts, JoinMe, Adobe Connect, and Skype so the team can meet virtually, but still have video and audio real-time connection with each other.

How Do We Make Hybrid Approaches Work?

Hopefully, most of the project management world has embraced Agile today and understands the need for its use in solving modern project management problems. Agile is the "elephant in the room" for doing project management. Yet, there is still a need and a place for using the tried-and-true traditional waterfall approach as well. Waterfall shouldn't be discarded and forgotten. But now, the hard part comes! How can we marry these two approaches and effectively use them together in projects and programs? I don't think this is going to be easy!

Many people in the Agile community think of "hybrid projects" in quite a negative way. They think a hybrid approach corrupts Agile and, therefore, should not be used. They would say if you attempt to mix Scrum and waterfall, you won't get "Scrum + water + fall," instead you will get "Scrum + water + fail!"[23] In large part, I don't disagree! If you attempt to use Scrum and waterfall/predictive approaches within the same portion of a project (or subproject; e.g., use Scrum, but also try to use a Gantt chart to define the critical path and schedule[24] for the next six to nine months), you will likely fail. But if you completely separate the waterfall/predictive pieces of the project (or subprojects) from the Scrum/Agile pieces and handle each independently of each other, then I think this can work and it makes sense to do so. In fact, it is often going to be necessary. In my experience, management within my own company would not allow me to use Scrum or Agile on all projects or (subprojects). It would be far too expensive. They would not support having dedicated teams of 5 to 10 senior engineers or "generalizing specialists" on all parts of my projects. Again, that would be far too expensive and impractical. I'm going to have to work hard to get their buy-in to use Scrum or another Agile method on some high-priority subprojects or portions of projects. Also, I'm going to have to work hard to educate them that, for these subprojects, they are going to have to be much more involved and they are also going to have to support a new culture.

Yet, this might be a hard sell to both the Agilists in our organization and those who favor the traditional approach. Some Agilists say that a company cannot adopt Agile halfway or part way and, therefore, can't allow for "hybrid projects." It's an "all or none affair." If you try to immediately use a hybrid approach, you will risk failing at adopting Agile. Your "Agile project" will fail, but it wasn't a defect in the Agile methodology, it was a failure in the way in which it was implemented.

---

[23] See *"What Is Hybrid Agile"*—https://vitalitychicago.com/blog/what-is-hybrid-agile/

[24] To be precise, we would use a "Network Diagram"— such as an Activity on Node (AON) Network Diagram—to show the critical path. A Gantt chart, in its original formulation, is only a bar chart and doesn't show dependencies or logic between activities like the AON diagram.

The Agilists will say this is almost like converting to a new religion and something we must do for the whole company! Obviously, that's very hard to do and it will be difficult for the organization to make this transformation. Jim Highsmith, one of the key authors of Agile articles and books, says, "Stop doing Agile. Start being Agile!" I believe a big part of what he means is that it's a mistake to adopt some pieces of Scrum and other Agile approaches (e.g., incorporating daily standup meetings, having an information radiator, calling your requirements the "Product Backlog"), but not fully embracing the entire Agile approach and culture. Of course, he means that the entire company must do this! He also means don't follow Scrum practices halfway, or in name only. Doing so is called being Agile in name only (AINO); yes, it is so common there is an acronym for it! In other words, don't do daily standup meetings, but make the daily standup meeting the same as the traditional weekly status meeting. Don't say you are going to adopt Agile, but then require that the traditional PMO policies stipulating the team must use MS Project to build a network diagram and define the critical path stay in place. (Don't do this for the parts of the project where you are using Agile.) Don't require all the normal project documents (all 30+ project documents defined in the Version Six *PMBOK® Guide!)* such as a risk register, stakeholder register, and issue log be developed. Yes, some may be needed, but these should be evaluated on a case-by-case basis. If they are needed, it should be because they provide value to the customer, which includes whether they are needed to meet regulations or standards the customer requires.

Far too many people say they are using Agile and they are totally on board with it, but then it turns out they are using it halfway or in a corrupted manner. So, the risk of this occurring is even greater when we venture out to use hybrid approaches. There is a real danger that we will not get the "best of both worlds," and instead get the "worst of both worlds!" Yet, there is a danger of this happening no matter what project management approach or methodology we use! PMs are always finding ways to *not* do communications well, *not* run meetings well, *not* obtain requirements, *not* plan well, *not* treat the team members well, or *not* pay attention to important contract obligations, and so on. Trying to follow a particular process or a methodology won't guarantee anything!

However, using a hybrid approach is about finding optimum ways of:

- Communicating well with our team members and customers
- Running efficient and effective meetings
- Obtaining requirements that add value for our customers
- Soundly planning and executing to deliver on features that add value to the customer
- Treating team members and other project stakeholders well, prioritizing them over processes and procedures
- Paying attention to important contract obligations, while effectively collaborating with the customer

There are two different ways of referring to hybrid Agile projects:

1. The first approach is not controversial, and it refers to mixing different Agile methodologies such as Scrum and XP within one project. This topic is worthy of a long discussion, and in fact, today, there is plenty of discussion on using hybrid approaches by scaling Agile methodologies throughout the enterprise, especially within programs. Two of the most popular frameworks for scaling Agile in a hybrid way are Scaled Agile Framework (SAFe) and Disciplined Agile Delivery (DAD). These frameworks are primarily focused on scaling Agile methodologies for software and IT projects and defining processes for using Scrum, XP, Lean, Kanban, and DevOps. However, a number of authors think SAFe and DAD impose too much structure, are too prescriptive, and therefore, are too restrictive. (For example, Googling "Does SAFe Agile impose too much structure" results in a number of articles that argue for this position.) Again, no one process or methodology fits all situations, and these frameworks may take away the freedom that project teams need for determining the right methodology in the right situation.

   Another objection that is often voiced is the idea that teams should give one methodology, for example, Scrum, a good nine months or longer before venturing out and mixing in other Agile methodologies. Key authors of Agile/Scrum articles say, "Yes, Scrum is easy to adopt, but it's hard to perfect and excel in using." So, give it a good try on its own with the basic team roles along with the basic meetings and rituals before venturing out and adding any other elements.

Lastly, I find it very interesting that neither SAFe nor DAD allows for integrating traditional waterfall approaches within the hybrid framework. Why wouldn't they allow for that? If some projects or parts of projects involve work we've done many times before and for which we have very good historical records of time and cost—if the customer knows in detail exactly what they want starting out—won't it be less expensive and more efficient to use a traditional waterfall approach for these parts? I think the answer is clearly, "Yes!" I think many of our projects, today, are large enough and complex enough that parts of the projects are work-packages that we have done many times before, and these parts are "cookie-cutter." It will be simpler, less expensive, and faster to handle these cookie-cutter parts with a traditional waterfall approach. We will expand on this discussion throughout this book.

2. The second meaning of "hybrid project management" is jointly using an Agile approach with a traditional waterfall approach within the same project, and this is the controversial topic. Can this be handled effectively? What are the key obstacles and challenges? As I've said, many people in the Agile community think it is foolish to attempt to do this! I think it is necessary in many corporate environments, today, and we need to find ways to make it work. I would like to argue that as long as the Agile components are kept separate from the traditional/predictive components, then this can work. What are the main difficulties? Let's go through the "Problem Areas for Agile" that we described in the previous section, and see how some of these problems map into managing a hybrid project, mixing components that are Agile with components being handled in a traditional/predictive way.
   - First and foremost, we said the right stakeholder relationships and culture in the organization must exist to support Agile. Agile is not as much a project management methodology for how to best obtain requirements and divide a project into phases or stages as it is a new culture and

mindset. To just make Agile work successfully on its own, as we've described, a culture of freedom and trust must be provided to the team members. Senior management must buy into this idea, understand they have a key role to play, and get at least a basic education in Agile. They must realize that they will need to be much more involved than they would in a traditional (waterfall) environment. So, to make hybrid work, where both programs and projects contain both traditional pieces and Agile pieces, is going to be even more challenging. I think it's going to be paramount to provide this "Agile culture" or "Agile mindset" across the entire hybrid project or program, not just the Agile pieces. It would be impractical and even offensive to handle some parts of the project or program with an entirely different management approach than other parts. Again, senior management and the entire company must be supportive and buy in to this idea. Also, everyone must understand it's a mistake to mix the two approaches together on the same subproject or portion of a project.

It may seem overly idealistic and utopian to provide this type of culture company wide, but it is very possible. In fact, many Tech companies such as Apple, Google, and Intel are doing this today. They are providing this culture of the "Agile mindset" throughout the company: in programs, projects, and even for operational functions.

Allowing for much freedom and trust for employees doesn't simply imply that one person's ideas are as good as everyone else's, that the employees are free to do whatever they want, or work on whatever they want! No, quite the contrary. It's understood that striving for value is paramount and we will use Lean techniques to quickly identify waste and remove it from the product backlog or work assignments. By using Agile and Lean, we are focusing even more efficiently on achieving value and eliminating waste than we would in a traditional company structure.

If the company's culture is to use Scrum (or another Agile methodology) on all projects, then it might be difficult to sell the idea of being flexible and allow some projects—or parts of projects—to use a traditional approach. Both senior management and the project management team members themselves might be pretty resistant to that idea. Likewise, if the company culture or the PMO culture is to use a waterfall approach and EVM on all projects, then it could be difficult to sell people on the idea of integrating in Agile for some projects or parts of projects. But, as I've said multiple times, it makes sense to be open-minded to this. We should recognize that there isn't one perfect process or approach for solving all problems. For almost any type of job, we have to learn what's the best tool and for what situation. So, everyone on the hybrid project needs to get basic training in the Agile method being used, and also basic training in the nuts and bolts of traditional project management and why it is still necessary, today. We need to send senior managers to this training, also!

- How do we organize all the different components in the hybrid program/project? How do we ensure the Agile components are managed separately from the traditional components, but all the pieces are integrated together cohesively? As we've described, many of our modern projects are big enough and complex enough that some parts of the project (some work-packages, if you will) are cookie-cutter, and it makes perfect sense to use the traditional waterfall approach for these parts. As we mentioned earlier, it's going to be less expensive and more efficient to let the classic fully empowered PM run the show, be accountable for all planning, all executing, and all monitoring and controlling. This PM will hand out parts of the PM plan to individuals on the team, will ensure they execute against the plan, and will also be accountable for measuring variance, measuring progress, and doing forecasting. Having a colocated team of 5 to 10 senior individuals dedicated to the project is a much more expensive option. This is especially true when we know, going in, exactly what the customer wants.

However, for the parts of the project where the customer does not know exactly what they want when starting out—and, there will be a premium on discovering requirements and a premium on creativity—one of the Agile approaches would be best. (This is also true for projects where some of the other risks we have discussed apply: "handling the half-baked idea" and "handling impossible constraints!")

How can we best integrate different approaches in a hybrid model? Ken Schwaber, in his book *Agile Project Management with Scrum,* describes an ingenious way of using Scrum all by itself for fairly large, complex projects. If we have a project that's large enough where we are going to need 50—or even more—project team members, then he says divide the project into multiple Scrum teams and divide the project work between these different teams. Then, to integrate and coordinate all this work and handle dependencies, have a representative from each Scrum team meet with the other teams in a "Scrum of Scrums" meeting. His graphic for this "Scrum of Scrums" meeting looks something like that in Figure 1.13.

The Scrum of Scrums meetings may function in a very similar way to the "daily standup meetings" of a normal Scrum process. But in the Scrum of Scrums meeting, the team members will only discuss stories or features where there are dependencies with stories and work the other Scrum teams are doing. Like a standup meeting, the purpose will be for each representative to provide their update/status to the other team's status and progress and also review dependencies between the teams' work.

Let's take this concept another step further. For the parts of the project—or subprojects or work-packages—that are being managed in a traditional waterfall way, why not allow the classic traditional PM, who is managing these subprojects, attend the Scrum of Scrums meetings to ensure coordination between these parts of the project and the other parts being handled with Scrum? To make sure all this works smoothly, the traditional PM will need to understand very well how Scrum works and why

- *Because Scrum is "lightweight," – many people think it is inappropriate for more complex projects.*
- *A possible solution is to divide the project into multiple Scrum teams, and then have representatives from each Scrum team attend "Scrum of Scrum meetings" to coordinate the activities in the different teams. The Scrum of Scrums will work much like the daily stand-up meetings, but perhaps not on a daily basis.*

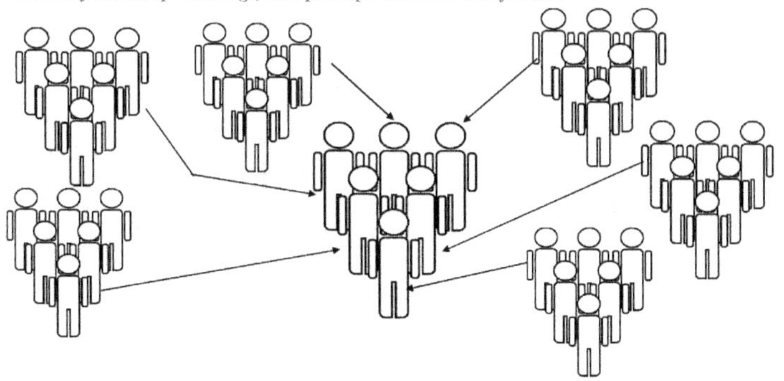

Figure 1.13 Scrum with complex projects?

parts of the project are being handled with Scrum. The Scrum Master representatives to this Scrum of Scrums meeting will need to understand why parts of the project are being managed in the traditional way and be tolerant and open-minded to that approach, as well.

Now, the graphic in Figure 1.13 looks like the one in Figure 1.14.

Does this "Scrum of Scrums" approach provide a ready solution for handling almost all large, complex projects where there are many stakeholders and stakeholder groups? Also, could we keep expanding on this idea, so that for even larger and more complex programs, we can go to a "Scrum of Scrums of Scrums" concept? No, I think there are limits to how far we should attempt to take this idea. We must still deal with the #1 Risk that we defined earlier: "Define scope so the approved requirements are SMART, but also where boundaries and exclusions are defined, and the stakeholders are all on the same page!" This is the hard part of project management. In Agile, we are transferring the primary responsibility for accomplishing this from the classic fully accountable PM to the product owner. But doing such a transfer doesn't readily solve the problem or simplify the difficulty of accomplishing this task. In a large, complex project or program with many stakeholder groups, we may need multiple product owners representing key functional business areas, and these product owners may have different needs and goals. There can be incompatibilities

- *We could try a hybrid approach, using the Scrum of Scrum approach, but for some sub-projects, we might have a traditional PM, and have the traditional PM attend the "Scrum of Scrum meetings."*

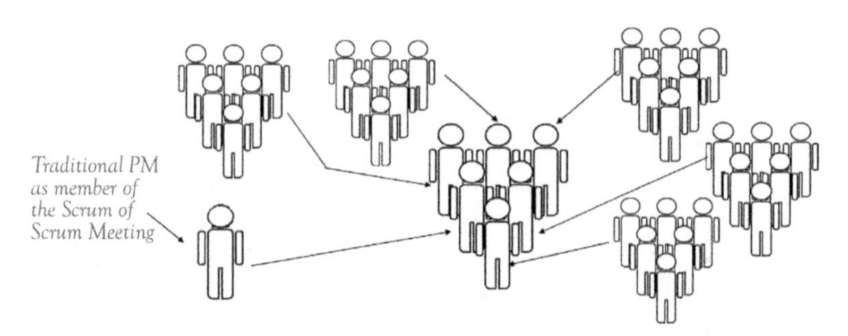

Figure 1.14 Hybrid project—mix of Scrum and traditional

at this level, and even different political goals in the organization. So, this could still be very difficult. When there are incompatibilities on the priorities of features, stories, and requirements, someone is going to have to be empowered to make the final decision. If almost all of the subprojects are being handled with an Agile methodology, then we are delivering incremental tangible value very quickly (in one- to four-week iterations), so that will make it much easier to see the value, and therefore, the priority of what is being created. But someone has to be either a fully accountable PM or a fully accountable product owner and make a decision on priorities and formally accept what is being created in the project. It's essential that the right product owner be chosen. You do not want to have a situation where four or five iterations have passed and the sponsor for the project vetoes what the product owners have approved, and we have to go back to square one.

One danger of trying to employ a "Scrum of Scrums" concept or multiple project teams—whether the teams are using an Agile approach or a traditional approach—is letting the number of Scrum teams or number of subprojects get out-of-hand. On the FBI Sentinel project, Sutherland said it was essential to reduce the number of stakeholders on the project, and a key part of their success when they adopted a Scrum approach was to reduce the staff from 220 to 40. Also, on the Medco project we previously mentioned, stakeholders were deadlocked on what should be included in the project and what the priorities of the requirements should be. When they adopted a Scrum approach for handling their "impossible constraint," they dramatically reduced the number of requirements and were able to get agreement on the priorities. On a hybrid project, it's still going to be essential to maintain focus on the "20 percent of the requirements that will meet 80 percent of the need." With multiple product owners representing different business groups, and with potentially 10 to 20 subprojects, this is going to be more difficult to accomplish than when we're managing one Agile project. Nevertheless, it's key that this be done.

- Lastly, if we use a Scrum of Scrums approach, or we have multiple subprojects, there needs to be independence between the subprojects and the Scrum teams. The teams need to be as self-directing as possible. If there are many dependencies between the subprojects and the subprojects are highly "coupled," then a predictive planning approach is going to be needed. In the 1970s, when I started my career doing systems design and programming, hot topics were "modular programming," "go-to-less programming," and "top-down design." An excellent book on this subject is *Reliable Software through Composite Design*, by Glenford Myers. A key point Myers made was that to successfully create reliable software, the program modules needed to be modularized in a top-down, hierarchical way and the modules needed to be as "loosely coupled" (or independent) as possible. This is very reminiscent of one of the key qualities of a well-written story—that it be independent of other stories and features. (This is part of the "INVEST" acronym for well-written stories. Stories should be *I*ndependent, *N*egotiable, *V*aluable, *E*stimable, *S*mall, and *T*estable.)

I said earlier that we must keep the parts of the project where we are using Agile totally independent and distinct from the parts where we are using a traditional or predictive planning approach, and I would like to make some qualifications. Though this is generally correct, there can be benefits in using some aspects of Agile on a traditional/predictive project, especially using Agile communication techniques such as a burndown chart or Kanban Board. Also, using Agile brainstorming techniques, facilitation techniques, and prioritization techniques can add a lot of value. In Chapter 3, we will explore in much more detail how Agile can add on key capabilities in processes defined in the *PMBOK® Guide* such as *Collect Requirements* and *Define Scope.* However, in other key ways, we need to emphasize and caution that it will be a serious mistake to try to require other elements of waterfall and predictive planning while we are doing Agile. For example, in the early planning stages for the Agile portions or subprojects, it is a mistake to try to put together a very detailed scope statement, a WBS with all deliverables decomposed down to level 4 or level 5, and a schedule with the critical path defined for the next six months out. Doing this is 180 degrees apart from how and why we use Agile. It would also be a mistake to have the classic fully accountable PM run the Agile parts of the project. We need to empower the team, let them choose what they will work on next out of the backlog, and make the team accountable for the project.

Chapter 1: Summary and Conclusions

I started off this book saying these are very interesting and challenging times for PMs. No pressure, but our companies are really depending upon us to help them survive in these difficult days: Tom Friedman's "Age of Accelerations."

I also said that project management is a difficult job, and I think that's an understatement. We never have all the resources we need or want for our projects, enough budget, or enough time. Worse, we never have all the power we really need to get agreement on key decisions and to keep the project moving forward as we envisioned. We are not kings or queens and we cannot force agreement on key decisions or legislate what the outcome will be. This is all about "people skills," "soft skills," and "herding cats." Many of us are managing large, complex projects and we are working with stakeholders who outrank us not only in our own organization, but also in external organizations. Nonetheless, it's up to us to get everybody onto the same page regarding the vision and requirements for the project and other key constraints. If we don't do this, the project will surely fail, and the blame will fall on us, not on the unreasonable, irrational stakeholders with all their different needs and different wants! If we can pull this off and manage this project to a successful conclusion, this will be amazingly rewarding. There might be more lucrative things to go do, but this will be very rewarding.

In today's IT-centric world and technology-centric world, "knowledge work projects" and software projects are the dominant type of project. Surveys of PMs in the Washington, DC PMI® chapter—the largest chapter in the world with over 11,000 members—in the past 5 to 10 years have indicated that more than 70 percent of our PMs are managing IT projects. And, by PMI's own surveys, they reported that more than 90 percent of all IT projects are being managed using one of the Agile methodologies. Agile is definitely critical for managing most projects today.

Nonetheless, I have argued there is definitely a time and place to use the traditional, and even waterfall, project management approaches. There is a lot of sound, core knowledge in the traditional approaches that should not be neglected. We should be big enough and open-minded enough to recognize this. There will be times when we need a fixed-price contract with our customer where all the I's are dotted and T's are crossed. In many of these situations, we will need to do predictive planning and use a waterfall approach. However, increasingly, our projects today are "knowledge work" projects, and we will need to discover and explore requirements as quickly as we can with short iterations. Agile methodologies will be the best choices in these situations. Lastly, many of our projects are large enough and complex enough that parts of the project should be handled with the waterfall approach and parts should be handled with Agile. No one process and no one methodology fits all situations. I am convinced that hybrid approaches will be increasingly important in the coming years.

I hope I've made that case for you too or, at least, provoked some questions and thought on this topic!

CHAPTER 2

Additional Thoughts on Agile and Hybrid Projects

Agile Contracts: Can Agile Be Used with Fixed Price Contracts?

Previously, we said Agile projects work best in the "Time and Materials" contract world and not fixed price. Why? Before we can explore this in more depth, let's first look at three of the basic contract types mentioned in the Version Six *PMBOK® Guide* (pp. 471–472) that students need to know for the PMP® Exam, which include

- Firm fixed price (FFP)
- Cost-reimbursable (CR; also known as "Cost Plus")
- Time & Materials (T&M)

- *Fixed-price Contracts*: Overview: In the fixed price world, the vendor bids a fixed price for the deliverables defined in the Statement of Work (SOW) and is responsible for any cost overruns, if necessary, to create the deliverables. Therefore, this is the riskiest contract type for the vendor: if there is any overrun, the vendor is responsible for 100 percent of the overrun. This also implies that going into the engagement, the customer knows in detail what they want and they will be choosing between vendors on price. The vendor needs a very detailed, lengthy SOW starting out so that they can predict accurately what their costs will be, and offer a price that has an adequate profit margin included. If the vendor bids a fixed price for a contract where the SOW is very high level and vague, then they are playing some sort of game—they are willing to lose money on this contract because they believe they will win a follow-on contract that is very lucrative)—or they are being very foolish. When the time comes for the customer to accept the deliverables, the customer can refuse to accept the deliverables as they are, and ask for more features. They can claim that as they understood the SOW, these features should have been included. If the SOW was high level and vague and the acceptance criteria were not clearly spelled out, then the vendor has no recourse, and must add in the extra features. This is the classic situation we described earlier that leads to what project managers hate most: Scope Creep!

- *Cost-reimbursable contracts*: For CR contracts, the situation is just the opposite from what we found with fixed price contracts. Now, the customer doesn't know exactly what they want or they only know what they want at a high level. They know business requirements or functional requirements, but not the detailed engineering design solution. They will want the vendor to create a new solution and determine the best detailed engineering design that will meet their functional requirements. Since they don't know exactly what they want going into the contract, they can't expect the vendor to bid a fixed price. Therefore, they tell the vendor that they will pick up all of the vendor's costs: their labor, tools and equipment, and some portion of their indirect costs. On top of this they will add profit. So, some people call the CR contracts "cost plus" contracts, which equates to cost plus fee, or cost plus profit. For the PMP® exam, students need to know three or four different variations of these CR contracts: Cost plus percentage of cost (CPPC), Cost plus fixed fee (CPFF), Cost plus award fee (CPAF), and Cost plus incentive fee (CPIF). Now, for CR contracts, the customer has the risk. If there is a cost overrun, if the vendor takes significantly longer to create the solution than what was first estimated, and the cost are far higher than what was first estimated, the customer is picking up all of these additional costs.

- *Time and Materials contracts*: For the federal government and for PMI®, Time and Materials contracts (T&M) are a mix of fixed price contracts and CR contracts or are "hybrid." There is truth to that statement, but the customer has far more risk with T&M contracts, and they resemble the CR world much more than the fixed price world. A customer would typically pick a T&M contract type when they do not know what they need created, and no specific deliverables are being defined at the outset. The customer wants to hire resources or rent tools and equipment and will manage these resources carefully to see that something of value is created. Perhaps you need a new website designed, but you don't know exactly what you want in this new website. So, you hire people who specialize in creating websites, and you agree to pay them on a T&M basis by the hour for their work. You will also pay for any tools, software or other equipment, and facilities that may be needed. When the vendor bids their hourly rate, they build profit into that hourly rate. Once the vendor bids their labor rates, those rates are fixed for the term of the contract. Hence, this contract type is part fixed price and part CR. The customer has the lion share of the risk. If the project goes on much longer than expected, you are picking up all of these costs.

Since the labor rates cannot be changed over the term of the contract, this contract is best used for a short duration engagement. If the contract spans a significant number of months, or even more than a year, the assumption is that new resources may need to be brought on, and their labor rates could likely be higher, but the vendor could not charge for those higher labor rates. So, PMI® would say that T&M should be used for very short duration engagements where the deliverables are undefined.

So, which of these three contract types is most suited for Agile projects? The answer is clearly T&M. The assumption for an Agile project is that the customer doesn't know what they want starting out. We will be exploring and discovering requirements as we move from iteration to iteration. We are handling the "Cone of Uncertainty" by using short iterations to explore requirements and use Lean to groom the value chain.

However, as we mentioned earlier, senior managers, and especially financial people, often have an unfavorable opinion of T&M contracts. The project manager often hears his or her sponsor say things like "I must have a firm end date for this project!" ... and "You know I don't have infinitely deep pockets." ... "This project cannot cost a dime more than _____ ×______ dollars!" So senior managers and customers are much more comfortable with the fixed price world. Can we give them a fixed price using Agile? The answer is clearly "yes!" We know the duration of each iteration (the length of the iteration was chosen upfront in release planning to be between one and four weeks). Additionally, we know the cost of each iteration, because we know the number of team members involved in each iteration, and we know their labor rates, so we can just multiply the labor rates of the resources by the duration of the iteration to get the cost. Suppose the cost of each iteration is $80,000, and we propose to senior management that we will do 10 iterations over 10 months (each iteration is one month). Therefore, we are giving senior management a fixed price for this release of $800,000. We propose this to our sponsor and other senior managers, but we also remind them that we are not promising exactly what we will create in the 10 iterations. That is to be determined (TBD).

But most Agile contracts are T&M, or some variation on the T&M theme. This could be T&M with a ceiling price, and the Dynamic Systems Development Method (DSDM) contract type is a common Agile contract that also incorporates aspects of T&M. The customer agrees to acceptance criteria which are quite high level, and not specific design requirements.[1]

[1] For more details on different contract types, see Chapter 3, "Procurement Management—Different Contract Types." We review other variations of Fixed price contracts (Fixed price incentive fee, FPIF; and Fixed price economic adjustment, FPEA); plus other CR contract types—CPPC, CPFF, CPAF, and CPIF. We also review some other Agile contracts, including DSDM contract, Graduated fixed price contract, and Fixed price work-packages.

"Money for Nothing and Change for Free" Contract

I think the most interesting of the Agile contracts is the "Money for Nothing and Change for Free" contract type that was invented by Jeff Sutherland. (Sutherland is having some fun with us, and the contract name is playing off the name of a song—"Money for Nothing"—from the 1980s by Dire Straits!) This contract type defines how we can achieve the best of the T&M world (discovering and exploring requirements in short iterations) and also give the customer and senior management the capability to do early kill-points, so they can control the price, too. Nonetheless, the vendor doing the project is protected even when an early kill-point is exercised. Here are the basics of this contract type:

- Customer and contractor agree on product backlog and relative weights of features/stories.
- During the project for any iteration (or Sprint), the customer can make any changes they want. But whatever new stories are added, then stories of equal weight are swapped out.
- The customer can terminate any time they want, but have to pay 20 percent of the remaining value of the project.

Here is an example Sutherland gives us for how this would work for an Agile software project.

> A construction company hires an Agile Software company to deliver an application within 20 months for $10M and decides to use one-month iterations. For the second and third iterations, the customer swapped out some stories for others they thought had more value. At the end of three iterations, the customer cancelled the project!
>
> The customer had paid $1.5M to the contractor for the first three iterations, and owed 20% of the remaining $8.5M, or $1.7M. The contractor had spent $1.3M on development, but received $3.2M. The contractor's projected profit percentage went from 15% to 60%! Even though the customer spent $3.2M for the

application, they had expected to spend $10M. They also received the application 17 months early.

This shows how using Agile and Lean and going after 20 percent of the requirements that will meet 80 percent of the customer's need in the first iterations, we can create something of high value in a fraction of the time, and for far less money than first anticipated. This validates how we can obtain a 300 percent improvement in productivity compared to a traditional approach. Clearly, this was a "win–win!"

Can Agile Be Used Effectively with EVM?

If you Google "How do I use EVM with Agile," you will get hundreds of hits, and 95 percent or more of these articles say "Yes, this is quite easy to do!" Within these articles, the authors will give you examples of how to do this. Even PMI® is totally on board with this whole concept. For their Agile certification exam—the PMI-ACP® (Agile Certified Practitioner)—they include questions of how to derive the four key EVM variables (PV, EV, AC, and BAC) in an Agile release. They give you story points actually being completed over time, you also know the number of story points planned for each iteration and the budget for each iteration.

So, being provided this data, we can define the values for the four EVM variables, but we are being misled. There is still a huge disconnect between using Agile and using EV. We have pointed out that EVM is closely aligned with traditional project management and the waterfall project lifecycle approach. Criterion number one in the current EVM specification clearly states:

Step 1: To the extent possible, you must define the full scope of the project. (Equates to EVM Criterion #1)

Fleming and Koppelman expand on this point later in their book, *Simple Earned Value on All Projects (Simplified Translations of the 27 EVM Criteria),* where they say,

> The first group of criteria deals with the requirement for any new project to be completely defined, and planned, prior to starting

> performance of the work. Today, we would typically call this effort defining the scope of the project. Think about it: EV Measurement cannot take place without some definition of what constitutes 100 percent of the project.

So, we're in the project world of "defined scope." Requirements are clearly and exhaustively defined in a predictive manner early in the project in the planning phases. The planning phases are completed before starting the construction or implementation phases. This describes a waterfall approach.

This is 180° away from the Agile approach. With Agile, we are discovering and exploring requirements (or the backlog items) as we move through the different iterations. Here is an excellent quote from Ken Schwaber, one of the originators of Scrum: "Scrum is about the art of the possible, not you give me what I paid for, when you said you'd deliver it."

In the "defined scope" world of EVM, we are assuming that the customer knows what they want going into the project and we will be able to determine all the requirements in detail. In the Agile world, the assumption is the opposite. We assume the customer doesn't know exactly what they want and they only know what they want at a high level—business requirements or functional requirements. Therefore, the team will need to discover and explore the best detailed engineering solutions that meet the high-level requirements as we move through the different iterations. We accept that there will be a lot of change in the different engineering solutions that are proposed as we move from iteration to iteration. Some requirements or backlog items will be discovered to not have value and they will be removed from the backlog; they will be replaced with new backlog items that we think will have more value. So, this is much more of a "T&M" world, and we are using Lean to explore requirements to "groom the value chain." Management has to accept that, and not demand a fixed schedule, a fixed budget, and defined scope. But as we said in the chapter on Agile Contracts, I think senior managers, especially financial managers, have a hard time accepting that the entire project or release will be done under a T&M basis. They can accept that a small piece of the project might be subcontracted to a vendor on a T&M basis, but not the entire project. I think their reaction to such a proposal would be, "No, I have to have a firm end-date for this project and a firm ceiling price. I do not have infinitely deep pockets!" So, it may be a hard sell, but we must convince them that if we use Lean and Agile properly, we will create something of higher value and in less time, than if we tried to plan everything perfectly up front. As Jeff Sutherland points out in *Scrum: The Art of Doing Twice the Work in Half the Time,* if Agile and Lean are used properly, you can achieve a 300 percent improvement in productivity.

With EVM, we need "defined scope," and we need a very accurate BAC at the beginning of the project. If we do not have that, then the performance indices (CPI and SPI) will mean very little, and that goes for our forecasts Estimate at Completion (EAC) and ETC as well. In the world where the customer doesn't know exactly what they want going into the project, and we are in a T&M world, we can't get an accurate BAC. How can I give you an accurate BAC when you don't know exactly what it is that you want? If we are about discovering and exploring the best solution that will best meet your business need, then I can't predict exactly how long this is going to take or how much it's going to cost. In this T&M environment, our BAC might have the accuracy of the ROM (rough order of magnitude) estimate. The accuracy of a ROM for PMI® is anywhere from –25 to +75 percent. This means that when the real costs are learned or the final cost for the project are learned, these real costs might be 25 percent less than the ROM or 75 percent more. If that's the situation that we are normally in when we are using Agile, then who cares if CPI is a number significantly below 1, such as 0.8? Who cares to know that we are 20 percent over budget when the original budget estimate could be off by as much as 75 percent? What is the saying for this situation? "This is garbage in and garbage out."

If BAC is only as accurate as a ROM, then I cannot get the most out of the usual EVM forecasts—especially, the EAC forecast. In the real world today, there are more than 25 different ways to calculate EAC. Every one of these EAC equations, except one, requires using BAC. And of course, we need an accurate BAC—a "definitive BAC" where the accuracy is between –5 and +10 percent.

So, using Agile, I can't get an accurate BAC and, therefore, I can't use almost any of the EAC equations. Management is more interested in our forecasts than anything else, so this is a major problem.

But I've overstated the case here! I might not be able to get an accurate BAC in the normal Agile project for the entire Release or set of Releases for a project, but I can get accurate estimates for the current iteration, or perhaps even the next iteration or two. Therefore, I might not be able to get an accurate EAC forecast, but I could derive three of the four EVM variables for the current iteration, and perhaps the next two iterations also. Therefore, I can calculate CPI and SPI for the current iteration and, again, perhaps for the next two iterations too. As we said already, Earned Value (EV) should be used very early in the project when we're less than 20 percent through the Release. If we see that CPI and SPI and our variances CV and SV are not good for the current iteration or the next iteration, then this is a big warning sign. As we have said, once you're more than 20 percent through the project, it is very difficult to make any significant corrective changes in CPI to improve the project and get it back on track. So, EVM techniques could be used effectively for the current iteration or the next iteration. But, do we really need EVM for doing this? I think Agile provides its own type of reports in the information radiator—in particular, the burndown chart and burnup chart—that actually give us the same type of information, but in a much easier to understand format.

Another Key Risk: Configuration Management

It is necessary on all projects, I think, that we do "configuration management" very well. This is true whether we are using an Agile approach, a traditional waterfall or predictive planning approach, or a hybrid approach. It is vital that we:

- Track the latest versions of all our deliverables, parts, and components—also, our plans, documents, and even our processes.
- Document all the interrelationships of parts, components, and products (e.g., document what parts and components work with what products).
- Document the reason(s) we made a particular change as well as when and by whom. What was the benefit or the reason for making the change?

- Document what other products, parts, components, plans, documents, and processes are impacted by this change.
- Know where the latest up-to-date configuration management information (version information) is stored.
- Ensure everyone on the project team is following the best practices of using this information and updating it appropriately (i.e., using the latest configuration management information when they are creating products, software, parts, plans, or documents).

It is my opinion that most PMs think of configuration management as belonging mostly to the classic "PMP® world": that it is most important for engineering projects, construction projects, waterfall projects, and predictive planning projects. "Dot all the I's and cross all the T's!" "The Devil is in the details." "Do in-depth documentation for the project" ... and so on.

Some of the most infamous stories of failed engineering projects (Airbus A380A wiring design) stem from poor configuration management. The lack of proper configuration management for the wiring design of the Airbus A380A resulted in schedule delays of several years in the delivery of the plane and losses in billions (in Euros) due to cancelled orders. The CEO of Airbus was fired over this incident. A positive story of configuration management done well begins in November 2009. PMIWDC was able to have Jorge Quijano, the executive vice-president of the Panama Canal Expansion project, come to speak to the Chapter. This was a $5 billion plus project that started in 2007, and the newly expanded canal was opened on June 26, 2016. At the time Mr. Quijano spoke to the PMIWDC, this amazing project was doing incredibly well: It was "On schedule, on budget, and was meeting scope and quality!" (This is hardly ever achieved for engineering projects this large!)

At the time of his presentation, they were so confident of completing the project on time, they planned to open the new canal on the 100-year anniversary of the original opening of the canal which would have been in August of 2014. Not the year's anniversary, but the exact day's anniversary!—(August 15, 2014). However, labor disputes and strikes interfered with their progress, and the new "Third Set of Locks Project" did not open until June 26, 2016.

At the conclusion of Mr. Quijano's presentation, someone in the audience asked, "To what would you attribute your success on this project?" "What factor was the key factor for being able to meet scope, meet quality and stay on schedule and budget?" As I remember Mr. Quijano's response, without hesitating a second, he said, "Well, we always knew that handling change management and configuration management were very important, but for this project, we knew we needed to build up our processes, and improve them to a much greater degree." "We took the *PMBOK® Guide* to heart!" "This was the most important factor, I think, in achieving our success!" (*Some paraphrasing has been used in characterizing his response.*)

With a background in software and information technology (IT), I'm reminded of the following situations:

- A programmer is fixing a bug or is adding an enhancement to a particular program or module. Suppose when the programmer goes to update the program, he does not use the latest version of code (perhaps because the latest version was not properly stored in the library; or its version was not updated properly; or the programmer did not follow the right processes, and didn't check the version carefully). He goes ahead and makes the change to the code, updates the version to reflect that it is now the most current version, and then he places the code/program back in the library. What did he just do? He has introduced a bug into the system, and it may be days, weeks, or longer before this bug is encountered. At that point, it will probably be very time-consuming and expensive to analyze what exactly happened and how it should be fixed. He also just erased other enhancements or bug fixes that other programmers had made to this program. He has introduced a cancer into the system that could be very hard to diagnose and fix.
- Just as we said earlier, when we encounter a defect or a bug, we should fix it immediately. Also, for tracking versions, and doing configuration management, we need to make all the version updates (configuration management updates) immediately. From the Palm PDA example, we know that if we wait a week to fix a bug in a program, it could take 24 times

longer to make the correction. This is true also for doing configuration management. If we wait a week to make the needed version updates, we will have to retrace our steps and rethink where and why we made the change that we did and reanalyze all the things impacted by this change. Mistakes will likely occur doing these updates!

- I was an "Escalation Manager" and "Operating Systems Specialist" for HP back in the late 1980s and early 1990s. For troubleshooting certain problems at that time, I might need to "dial" into a customer's system, check the version of their operating system (OS), the file system, and other subsystems to diagnose a recent system failure. Suppose in the analysis process, I believe I have identified the root cause of the failure and I conclude that a certain OS patch is needed. Then, suppose I download the wrong version of the patch to the customer's system! Suppose I did not do the configuration management checks that were necessary and failed to realize that the patch I downloaded was incompatible with the database software they were running, or possibly other subsystems. What did I just do? I've taken a "Hot Site" and turned it into "Chernobyl!" It is extremely important to do configuration management very well for this type of job, too.
- XP is the second most popular of all Agile methodologies, but is only used for software. XP emphasizes processes and best practices for developing software, and one of these best practices is *Continuous Integration.* Developers check in their code multiple times a day for testing, and this also tests to ensure their code is consistent with other code in the library. A central part of continuous integration is also version management.[2] As the code is tested and checked into the library, the version of the software is updated, and version control is maintained. Martin Fowler writes:

---

[2] For more information on Continuous Integration and its importance for software development, please see the article by Martin Fowler "*Continuous Integration.*" https://martinfowler.com/articles/originalContinuousIntegration.html

"The obvious (we hope) solution is to use a configuration management (source control) system as the source of all code. Configuration management systems are usually designed to be used over a network and have the tools that allow people to easily get hold of sources. Furthermore, they also include version management so you can easily find previous versions of various files. Cost shouldn't be an issue as CVS is an excellent open-source configuration management tool."

"For this to work, all source files should be kept in the configuration management system. "All" is often more than people think. It also includes build scripts, properties files, database schema DDLs (Data Definition Languages) install scripts, and anything else that's needed to build on a clean machine. Too often we've seen code controlled, but not some other vital file that has to be found."

- Lastly, when I updated all my PMP® Prep course materials for the Version Six update to the *PMBOK® Guide* (this entailed thousands of hours of work updating slides, quizzes, exercises, and videos for virtual training), every time I realized I needed to make a fix, an update, or a change to a slide, if I didn't do it immediately, and if I waited days to make the fix, then I was faced with a lot of extra work trying to remember exactly what needed to be fixed, why it needed to be fixed, and all the other content for the course that was impacted by the change as well. This could be amazingly labor intensive! If I pulled the wrong version of course materials and did not update the latest version, I, too, had introduced a cancer into all the course materials that would be very expensive and time-consuming to fix!

The bottom line, I think, is that configuration management is very necessary and must be planned for and followed on any project. This is true whether the project is an Agile software project or if we are creating or updating course materials, writing a book, building the Panama Canal, or building a new office building (and ensuring the BIM team design is "clash free" with the engineering design). Configuration management is essential for any project and illustrates where traditional, more formal project management processes intersect with the modern Agile best practices.

Complexity on Projects: Where Does Agile Help? Where Is a Predictive Planning Approach Needed?

Managing complexity on projects overlaps heavily what we said about managing risk. If there is high complexity, there is high uncertainty and, therefore, also high risk. We can mean a number of different things when we describe a project as being complex. This may mean:

1. We are managing a very large project with many stakeholders and stakeholder groups, for example, the FBI Sentinel project discussed earlier in Chapter 1.
2. We are managing a project with very difficult technical challenges to overcome in designing the correct product or solution, for example, the Wright Brothers' airplane or the 1960s Apollo mission to the moon.
3. We are managing a project in which politics plays a role in dealing with stakeholders, for example, the attempts to negotiate a Middle-East peace treaty.
4. We are managing a project where we just don't know what the solution will be and where a conceptual breakthrough is needed! For example, in physics today, the attempt to resolve the incompatibility between quantum mechanics and general relativity or solving a difficult mathematical problem like Fermat's Last Theorem.

Therefore, it makes sense that the different types of "complexities," described above, do map nicely into the RBS categories presented earlier: Business Risks; Product/Technical Risk; Project Risk; and Organizational Risk. It is not a perfect match, but I think there is definitely some correlation. The first example maps into the "Business Risk" and "Organizational Risk" categories fairly well; the second example maps into the "Product" or "Technical" risk category; the third into "Organizational risks"; and the fourth into "Product or Technical Risk."

In these different examples, where can Agile help us, and where would a predictive planning approach be more appropriate? I think for any case where prototyping will be helpful, Agile can be beneficial. We might think of these prototypes as "risk spikes" or "architectural spikes." Spikes are a new and interesting concept employed in Agile. These are a special experiment or an iteration to test the probability of a threat (negative risk) occurring, and reducing that probability. Similarly, "architectural spikes" are also used with Agile, and these are usually a special iteration or test of a hardware configuration, a software solution, or a design approach.

For the second example, before they tried to create a powered flight solution, the Wright Brothers spent several years experimenting—and testing (first with kites and then with gliders) different designs and ways to control an aircraft in all three important dimensions: pitch, yaw, and roll. Compared to the other pioneers at the time, their achievements can be attributed to their success in doing these experiments! Weren't these experiments really prototypes? Okay, they weren't accomplished in very short one- to four-week time frames, but nonetheless they were prototypes. Also, the Wright Brothers didn't have computer-aided design (CAD) technology available or our other modern IT technical capabilities. If they had these capabilities and also had the financial resources provided to some of the other pioneers in flight like Samuel Langley, they would have performed their experiments much more quickly.

Even for very difficult conceptual problems (e.g., a difficult problem in math or science), some form of "prototyping" or experimenting with ideas might be in order. A hallmark of scientific research today (or research in medicine or many other areas) is that there is far more collaboration between scientists and researchers than there was just a few decades ago. When a discovery is made, or some other breakthrough, teams of scientists from all over the world are quickly notified, and are often working together on the discovery or breakthrough. Isn't this Agile like? There is a lot of discovery, exploration and creativity involved. The scientists and researchers are not following a precise, predictive process. This isn't a waterfall, predictive planning project. To completely solve the problem may take years, but within that overall "program," there are many Agile like projects to make incremental advances.

However, with that said, oftentimes for solving difficult complex problems, a significant amount of time must be invested in upfront planning. In the late 1970s, when I started my career as a systems analyst/programmer, we would say the worst mistake a programmer could make would be to immediately start writing code. The inevitable result would be "spaghetti code," a mess of thousands of lines of tangled code that would be very difficult to debug or to understand! We would say it paid huge dividends to take more time upfront, plan and design the program, and "do it right!" We said, if the time to write a program was estimated to be at least a month, it would pay to spend at least half of that time planning and designing the program. The resulting program would be much cleaner (far fewer bugs), much easier for others to understand, and much easier to maintain. In the end, the program would be finished much more quickly. If we spend days of time (or weeks or months or longer) scratching out ideas on paper before starting to create our project's deliverables or we spend a lot of time visualizing the solution, then perhaps that's akin to doing tests and spikes. But this is also a core part of doing traditional upfront, intensive planning for a project.

So, isn't a long-term effort to solve a difficult problem in medicine (e.g. – find a vaccine for the COVID-19 virus, or find a solution to an intractable problem in physics) really a program that is hybrid? I think so. There will be Agile projects and subprojects within the program where there is a tremendous emphasis on creativity and discovery, and where no precise process is being followed.[3] There will also be parts where the team is doing due-diligence, following mandated regulations and processes, and following a prescribed plan. If you ask what's the ideal way to run such a hybrid program or project, you're going to be disappointed! The answer is that answer we often get that we may not like: "It depends!" As project managers and program managers we're being paid to think on our feet, and figure out the best way to run this hybrid program!

Virtual Agile Teams—Susan Parente

As part of the PMP® Certification, we learn methods and techniques for efficient and effective Agile project management. How do we use these

[3] As Doug DeCarlo says in *Extreme Project Management*, this akin to quantum physics, not classical physics!

when our team is not colocated? The intention of this section is to discuss how this can be done in a way that is still supportive of the Agile Manifesto and its principles and practices that we know and hold dear!

In our current age of social networking and global business, knowing how to work with virtual teams is becoming a necessity for Agile projects, instead of an exception. How can we use the project management methodologies in our toolbox to support high-performing virtual Agile teams? This chapter will address the need for virtual Agile teams and the tools to use for virtual Agile project management.

A virtual project is a project whose team members (all or some) are virtually located. Virtual teams have members who are not located in the same physical space (not colocated), meaning they are geographically dispersed. The team members may also be dispersed across boundaries of time, space, organization, or culture. These team members are connected either via a private network or the Internet. Team members are able to collaborate with each other and work together to deliver project objectives. When a virtual team is using the Agile approach for project management, they are considered a virtual Agile team. Here are some key definitions and concepts for virtual Agile:

- Virtual project: A project where the team members are dispersed and working together on a temporary endeavor, which delivers on a unique product, service, or result.
- Colocated team: A team that shares the same workspace.

I have worked on many Agile teams, some of them in a lead position and some of them as a team member. It is important to do Agile in a "colocated fashion" even when team members are virtual. How do we do that? For example, having the daily standup meeting via video conference, so everyone can see each other during the meeting. This also helps the development team build rapport with each other. It is extremely important for virtual teams to have a sense of trust between members. Trust is equally as important for colocated teams, but it is generally easier for them to achieve. For virtual teams, an effort needs to be made to establish trust with virtual team members. Video conferencing can assist with this, as individuals can both see and hear the other person, giving them an opportunity to see visual cues, body language, and so on. I have also found it easier to comprehend someone with an accent, if I am able to see them while they are speaking.

Understanding how trust is built and how it is evaluated is important for us to build team trust. The Trust Quotient is a great way for us as team members, as team leaders, or as a team to evaluate our trust level. The Trust Quotient is:

Trust = (Credibility + Reliability + Intimacy) / Self-Orientation*

*Trusted Advisor (n.d.) *The Trust Quotient and the Science Behind It*, Retrieved from https://trustedadvisor.com/why-trust-matters/understanding-trust/the-trust-quotient-and-the-science-behind-it

Increased team trust leads to increased team performance! Here are some ways that team members may build trust with one another:

- Build integrity with the team, by doing what you say and saying what you do. (The daily standup meeting supports team members' integrity with themselves and the team!)
- Be accountable for the work you do on the team. This doesn't mean you are to blame if something goes wrong, but it does mean finding a way to get the work done that you have agreed to do. This may mean getting other team members to assist you when you are stuck or struggling. Too often team members struggle in secret. Then pretend things are on course, or all is going well, when reaching out to the team for help is needed.
- In addition to asking for help, when you need it, keep an eye out for team members that are struggling and consider how you may assist them.
- Support and encourage team members and make sure they are acknowledged for the work they have done, are doing, and plan to do. (Everyone on the team has a role, and acknowledging everyone for the work they do builds trust.)
- "Stop and smell the roses…" It is unfortunate that one should need to be reminded of this. This is one of the main goals of the retrospective, but too often I hear this critically important

meeting turn into the blame game... Continuous improvement is not only about fixing things that aren't working (improving in challenging areas); it is about recognizing what *is* working and emphasizing it more!
- Team building isn't about "team-building exercises." It is about creating a supportive, positive environment where teammates have a place to grow and are allowed to fail and learn from failure. This is what team building is about. It is not about completing text book exercises on "team building."
- Realize that not everyone on the team will be happy at every moment of the project; however, using the boundaries created in the team charter, along with following the principles and practices of Agile, the team can be well supported.
- Don't take it personally... Team members should focus on what is valuable to the customer and the vision for the project, the iteration, and whatever they are working on. When things are not personal, it is easier to hear others' opinions and do what is best for the team and the customer.
- Create an environment of gratitude. An attitude of gratitude supports creativity, acknowledgment, team performance, and it develops trust!

As previously discussed, trust is an important aspect of Agile. As you may recall from earlier in this book, the Agile Ethos focuses on providing freedom and trust to the team members.

Agile Team Charter

One key element of Agile team development is the team charter. The team charter addresses team communications, answering such questions as:

- What is the preferred communication method for ad hoc communications?
- What are the response time expectations to Internet Messaging (IM), email, or voicemail (VM)?

- What is the escalation procedure if no response is received in the expected time frame?

The team charter should address these team communications and how to handle situations where the team is geographically dispersed across time zones, distance, or even time frames of when they work. (For example, some team members work 6 a.m. to 2 p.m., and others work 10 a.m. to 6 p.m. in the same time zone.) Can the team find enough overlap in working time where the team can do standups and operate in a colocated way? Working times should be fair, so that some team members are not overburdened. For example, one of the global Agile teams that I worked on had our meetings at 7.30 a.m. Eastern Time (ET), so it was 6 p.m. India Standard Time (IST). I have had other experiences leading global teams where I had meetings at 7 a.m. ET and 11 p.m. ET, to work with team members in Colorado and India. In Agile, it is essential to invite other stakeholders (beyond the team members), the project sponsor, customer, vendors, others, to informally come by the work area of the team and discuss things.

Virtual Agile Tools

With a virtual team, we need to make sure there is a way for stakeholders to be connected and involved with the work of the virtual team. Tools like Trello, Jira, and a home-grown Kanban Board (task board) using MS Excel may be used by the team and shared with the project stakeholders. These may be part of your team's information radiator and should be shared with the project stakeholders, not only the virtual team. This can be shared through an internal (Intranet or organizational website) or external (Internet) website. Another way that an information radiator can be shared is through SharePoint or other document management systems.

Meeting tools are essential for virtual teams. Of course, there is the tried and true teleconference call. This can work well, but with teleconference calls, one cannot share their screen, presentation, or even their visual cues. Also, if you are working with people around the globe, you may not want to pay the high prices for international calls. I work with people in India, Canada, Finland, Mexico, and many other locations. I don't want to pay high phone bills and international calling on my mobile phone, so

I use Skype to call these team members. (Sometimes I used video calling and sometimes I just used audio without video for calls.) Calling internationally is one of the benefits of using web-conferencing applications for virtual meetings. Other options for video conferencing software include Zoom, Cisco WebEx, GoToMeeting, Adobe Connect, Google Hangouts, and JoinMe. There is no shortage of options for virtual meetings. Pricing, performance, and features (for example recording, breakout rooms, chat features, drawing functionality, participant tools) are often the most important criteria when selecting a video conferencing software.

As a consultant, I use the software that my customer prefers, but my preference is for a software that has zero interruptions/connection problems, has recording capability, allows me to see multiple parties at once, and share my presentation as well as IM chatting functionality. For standup meetings, it is particularly important for all meeting attendees to be able to see each other. I tell my team that I don't care about their attire (sweatshirts and t-shirts work) and it is important for team members to be able to see each other when we are meeting. This virtual face time builds trust which, as discussed, is essential for virtual Agile team performance.

One thing to avoid is a connection that comes in and out (this is distracting for all attendees and frustrating for the person who is having connection issues). Obviously minimum Internet bandwidth requirements need to be met; however, some video conferencing software is better at managing this than others. I have found if video goes, but audio is still present, it is much less interruptive and more workable in a meeting. Another thing to look for is ease of use for new participants. Sometimes attendees might not be meeting regulars and you don't want to spend a significant amount of time getting them up to speed on the software used for the meeting. It should be easy for them to get onto the meeting and obvious how to mute their audio. Background noise is also a big challenge for both video conferencing and teleconference calls. I always ask people to mute their line when they are not speaking. Even as a meeting facilitator, I follow this advice. Of course, this leads to the problem of a person being muted and not realizing this or knowing how to unmute themselves. I find it valuable for the meeting administrator or facilitator to be able to mute all lines and unmute people, as needed, in addition to participants being able to do so themselves.

In general, the biggest challenges I have had with virtual meetings have not been the tools, but instead the participants. Having ground rules like:

- Arriving at least five minutes early.
- Muting when not speaking, giving everyone time to speak.
- Announcing oneself in chat or verbally when you join late (this is especially critical for teleconference meetings, as you often cannot tell someone has joined, except for a beep sound).
- Making sure your video is on, not just audio (often people have video locked down on their computer); allowing for video connection is important for the team to feel connected and have face time with each other.

All of this should be laid out in the communication section of the virtual Agile team charter. It is not that there is a right way to do any of this, nor is there a best tool, but instead it is important to include the team in creating the rules of team engagement, especially around virtual communication. If the team creates the rules and agrees to them, there should be little resistance in following them.

Agile Team Development

How does an Agile team develop in a virtual environment? Team development is the same in either a colocated or virtual environment; however, development for a virtual team is often more challenging. This is because ad hoc meetings are less likely to occur and there are fewer organic opportunities for team camaraderie. Fundamentally, to support team development in a virtual environment, we need to create opportunities that naturally occur when teams are colocated. For example, some teams have an open web conference connection in a meeting room or in a common workspace area (e.g., where the project task board or Kanban Board is located). As team members work throughout the day, they can see team members in other locations and update the task board in real time. I find this particularly valuable for teams where there are few members who are virtual and some team members that are colocated. Having a web conference line that is always open supports the virtual team members in feeling connected to those that are colocated.

Another idea is to have a video conference call standup meeting each morning. As a best practice, this is a 15-minute meeting. The "virtual standup meeting" should be executed in the most effective way for video conferencing. For example, many "virtual standup meetings" are done with the team sitting in their virtual offices in front of their computer. This is ok, as long as the meeting stays within the 15-minute timebox requirement. The purpose of people standing is so people don't get comfortable, settle in and have the meeting take more than the allocated time of 15 minutes. I know many people do a 15-minute phone call meeting; however, it is not the same. I know myself that I can get distracted when on the phone and start checking email. That is not good for keeping the daily standup meeting focused and valuable. A video call keeps everyone audibly connected and it is very valuable to see one another. I recommend sharing with everyone that their attire is not critical. Sweatshirts and hats are perfectly acceptable for a virtual team standup meeting. I know when I meet with clients via a video conference, I make sure I am dressed appropriately; however, I have met with many colleagues of mine wearing a fleece pullover or sweatshirt (especially in the winter). When meeting with your virtual Agile team, it is about staying connected with one another and being comfortable with one another, so I recommend business attire not to be a requirement. Trust is also very important for teams. As we've pointed out in numerous places in Chapter 1 of this book, it is essential for Agile projects to provide an environment of freedom and trust to the team members. This is a critical part of the Agile culture or "Agile Ethos." As previously stated, this also aligns with creating a "Theory Y" type of environment. When our team members are spread out in a virtual environment, trust is even more challenging to achieve, so even more effort and focus need to be placed on accomplishing this. Building team trust is important for all team development and it is critical for virtual teams. Agile teams support self-leadership and team learning. Since Agile teams often do not have a team leader, trust among team members can be even more important to the self-organized team. As previously stated, team trust is critical for virtual teams, as virtual team members are not face-to-face with their coworkers on a daily basis. Spending face time on a daily basis builds team trust. Given that, it is a best practice to have virtual team members meet face-to-face, when the team is initially formed, if it is possible. In particular, it is best to start a project with a face-to-face kickoff meeting. If that is not possible, consider a virtual video conference meeting for the project kickoff, so team members can see one another.

Project Planning for the Virtual Agile Team

How do we address these challenges of a virtual Agile team when planning for a project? Remember, in Agile, teams are self-organized. This does not preclude planning or structure for teams. A team charter is a great way to ensure all team members have the same understanding of the team's purpose and how the team will work together. It also establishes boundaries and ground rules on how team members work together. A team charter should be developed at the initial stage of team development (formation), when team members first start to work together on the project. It is a best practice for the self-organized team to develop the team charter in a group session. Doing this supports understanding of the value and purpose of the team charter and supports buy-in by team members. Ultimately, the team should decide how it is best for them to work together.

Since the Agile team members should be skilled in a number of roles, neither an organizational chart nor a Responsibility Assignment Matrix (RAM) are used for Agile projects. However, there are some project team development activities used for traditional projects that we want to also use for virtual Agile projects. These include:

- Orientation/training
- Team-building activities
- Setting ground rules or operating guidelines (this is included in the team charter)
- Setting Technology/ Use Protocols (this may be included in the team charter)

All of these activities are best practices to use for virtual Agile team development. It is important to recognize that much about virtual Agile team development is not different from traditional team or colocated

Agile team development. However, the way these activities are traditionally performed may be different when the team is not colocated.

Building Team Trust

Why is team trust critical for Agile projects? A major part of team development is the development of trust among team members. Trust is foundational to all relationships, and teams are a relationship of relationships. Given this, how can we build team trust for our Agile team? When developing trust, start with one's self, move to relationships with others on the team, and so on, growing your capabilities for developing trust.

Here is the Stephen Covey model, which he calls "The 5 Waves of Trust":

Trust Level	Description
Self	Trusting myself and my credibility. This is about integrity and being of one's word. This can be summarized by doing as I say and saying as I do
Relationship	My behavior with others. Without trusting myself, I cannot expect others to trust me
Organization	Aligning with my organization
Market	Trusting my organization's reputation
Societal	Making contributions in the world*

See the following video link for additional details on the 5 Waves of Trust from Stephen Covey's book *Speed of Trust*: http://youtube.com/watch?v=HjMNWr_qqfM

*Covey, S., (2009), "The 5 Waves of Trust." Retrieved from http://youtube.com/watch?v=HjMNWr_qqfM

There is much information about self-organized Agile team development, but team trust is critically underlying for this. This trust is even more important for virtual Agile teams. Consider that when you do not see people on a regular basis (or perhaps have not ever met them) it may be difficult to trust them. How do you know your team member will do what they said they will do and when they said they will do it? Team members must first be trustworthy, themselves, and then in relationships, to be trustworthy to their team. When a team has trust, they are able to move through the levels of team development more quickly and become a high-performing, self-organized team!

Managing the Virtual Project Team

Just as with traditional project management, virtual Agile team management includes conflict management, problem solving, and team leadership. Virtual project team management involves the following for both individual members and the team: meetings, performance, team goals, methods of communication, managing schedules, and managing team member interdependencies.

When managing the virtual project team, virtual communication and the use of virtual Agile tools are fundamental. Tools used for communication include:

- Hardware
- Personal computers (PCs)
- Connection including telephony, local area network (LAN), wide area network (WAN)
- Software: a variety of applications are used for communication
- Physical/media: paper, whiteboards, sticky notes, business cards, marketing material

Communication tools may entail software, hardware, or a combination of both. The following link provides an example of Cisco's Telepresence (software/ hardware) teleconference system: http://youtube.com/watch?v=0kd2SO1_kSA*

*Arnold, J. (12/6/06) "Cisco Telepresence Demo" Retrieved from: http://youtube.com/watch?v=0kd2SO1_kSA

The Virtual Communications Tool Map diagram (Figure 2.1) shows a number of virtual tools that may be used for virtual Agile project team communication. Diagrams like this may be used to select communication tools for the virtual Agile team. Space and time are on the axes of this chart. Space entails everything from colocated to virtual, which includes teams that may be partially colocated and partially virtual. On the X-axis is time from synchronous (same time or real time) to asynchronous. Keep in mind that even colocated teams may operate asynchronously if team members work at different times. The left side of the chart's focus is on

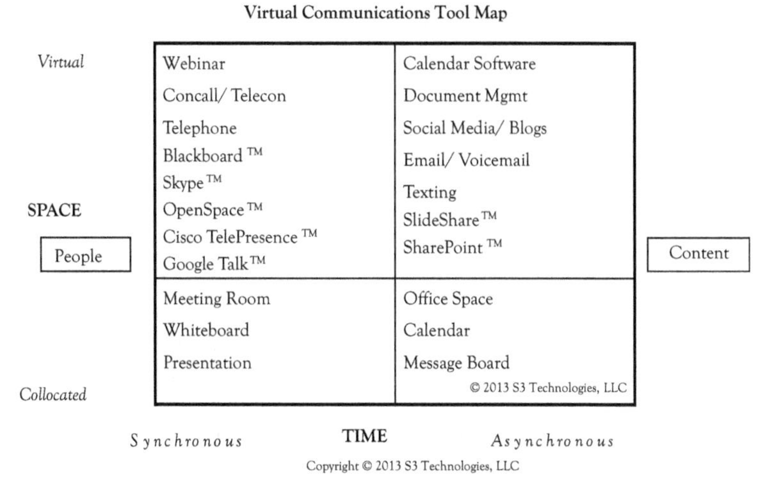

Figure 2.1 Tools for managing virtual projects

people and the right side focuses on content. The selection of communication tools considers both people and content. Too often I see virtual Agile teams select communication tools based on the "latest and greatest" tools, instead of basing their selection on the people, content, and needs of their virtual team. Doing this is like going grocery shopping for food without knowing who will be coming for dinner and what you would like to have on the menu. We may think of this as the virtual team's requirements gathering process for communication tools. The diagram above is a sampling of virtual communication tools, but certainly not a full list of possible tools. New virtual communication tools are developed regularly.

The above tools are not focused on Agile specifically; however, even Agile-specific tools should not be selected just because they are for Agile or even if they are specifically for virtual Agile teams. Communication tools should be selected by the team, for the team. This means they should be selected based on the team's needs with regard to space and time (which encompass people and content to be shared). You may see, in the figure, how computers and cloud storage are in both virtual and colocated space and in both synchronous and asynchronous time. When we are in real time (synchronous) the focus tends to be on people, whereas in asynchronous time, it is about content. Both are important to consider for any virtual Agile team.

When selecting communication tools for a virtual Agile team, consider using a SWOT (strengths, weaknesses, opportunities, threats) analysis of the virtual Agile project team. Virtual communication tools should play to the team's strengths, support its weaknesses, result in benefits from opportunities being realized, and reduce issues from threats being realized.

Best Practices for Virtual Agile Project Teams

Now that we have discussed virtual Agile team development and management, we are ready to discuss how to implement best practices for virtual Agile project teams. Our goal is to create extraordinary virtual project teams!

Here are some best practices for virtual Agile teams:

- Regular team meetings: meeting daily or weekly
- Weekly communication: via phone or web conference or via email communication
- Face-to-face meetings: The project kickoff meeting should be face-to-face, unless this is not possible. For global teams, this might not be possible. In situations where a face-to-face kickoff meeting is not possible, it is highly recommended to have a web conference meeting, where team members are able to see each other through video Internet connection. After the project starts, quarterly face-to-face meetings are ideal. At minimum, it is recommended to meet in person at least bi-annually or annually.
- Using professional tools: These help the team structure better workflows and improve team collaboration. Since the team is not colocated, it is more dependent on software tools to support communication, workflow, and team collaboration.

Team Consensus

Team consensus is about team agreement. Consensus is achieved by finding a proposal, direction, or solution that everyone can support or at least accept. This means team members need to consider how it will affect the team, not just themselves. Team members may not favor the consensus decision or approach, but they may agree to accept it as the best choice for the team.

Team consensus adds value and promotes team building and team development. It is important to listen to the perspective of ALL team members, especially those who are NOT in agreement. All members' concerns should be addressed and the decision should be modified, as needed. The end result should be a win–win for the team and it should be a creation of the team.

Managing Performance from a Distance

For virtual Agile teams, team management is only part of the picture. Our ultimate goal is to develop and support high-performing teams. How does one do this when their team is virtually located?

Fisher and Fisher address the challenges of virtual team performance with their Six-Step Goal-Setting Process, which entails Defining KPIs (Key Performing Indicators)/KRAs (Key Responsibility Areas), Identifying Benchmarks, Measuring Current Performance, Setting Goals, Clarifying Accountabilities, and Tracking and Communicating Results. (Figure 2.2)

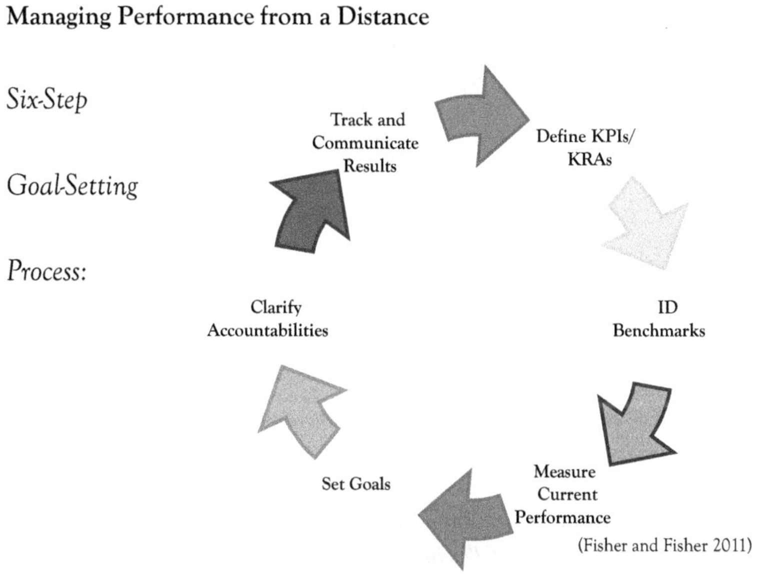

Managing Performance from a Distance

Six-Step Goal-Setting Process:

Track and Communicate Results

Define KPIs/ KRAs

ID Benchmarks

Measure Current Performance

Set Goals

Clarify Accountabilities

(Fisher and Fisher 2011)

Figure 2.2 Virtual project management: best practices

Summary—Virtual Agile Projects

How do we support the benefits of colocated teams in a virtual Agile environment?

At first sight, a virtual Agile team sounds like a dichotomy. Most Agilists think teams should be colocated. In practice, this is a fundamental part of the Scrum method. So, why talk about virtual Agile teams? They say that necessity is the mother of invention. While training professionals in Agile, I've had many people ask me how Agile practices and techniques work in a virtual environment. The reality is that there are teams working virtually and using Agile practices for project management.

For Agile teams, it's important for the team to find the best ways to work together. The team charter is an essential part to ensure team success in virtual Agile projects. Certainly, a virtual environment provides more challenges to the team than being colocated, but that does not mean the team cannot work together virtually, with the same level of productivity and performance that a colocated team has. This section's focus was on virtual Agile project management and how virtual and Agile work together. As discussed, this can be done in a way that is still supportive of the Agile Manifesto[4] and its principles and practices, which we know and hold dear! In our current age of social networking and global business, knowing how to work in a virtual team environment is a necessity on almost all projects: both Traditional and Agile. This is the rule, not the exception!

[4] The Agile Manifesto of 2001 is: www.agilemanifesto.org
Individuals and interactions over processes and tools
Working software over comprehensive documentation
Customer collaboration over contract negotiation
Responding to change over following a plan
That is, while there is value in the items on the right, we value the items on the left more.

CHAPTER 3

Overview and Thoughts about the *PMBOK® Guide*. Does Agile Fit in Well with the *PMBOK® Guide*?

Overview of the *PMBOK® Guide*

I obtained my PMP® certification in 1995. I volunteered in the Washington, DC PMI Chapter (PMIWDC) from 1996 through 2017 and was the trustee for the Chapter from 2009 to 2013. I have followed the evolution of the *PMBOK® Guide* from the draft of Version One—released in 1994—through Version Six—released in September of 2017. I have been teaching PMP® Prep classes as my full-time occupation since 2007. Also, I taught PMP® Prep classes for PMIWDC as a volunteer a couple times a year from 2003 through 2007. Here, I offer some thoughts and reflections on Version Six of the *PMBOK® Guide*—what I think is important and valuable in the book, what is extraneous, and the key things that are missing. I will continue with themes and points made previously in the book as well as discuss how and where Agile approaches expand upon some core ideas in the *PMBOK® Guide*. Additionally, I will discuss places where Agile is not a great fit.

The *PMBOK® Guide* is the primary reference book students use to prepare for the PMP® exam.[1] However, many students are very surprised to learn that the exam is not based *only* on this book. Indeed,

---

[1] By the way, as of January 2020—there are now more than 1 million certified PMPs worldwide.

test questions on the exam can come from anywhere in the "*PMBOK!*" What the heck is that supposed to mean? What is the *PMBOK?* Well, "***PMBOK"*** stands for "Project Management Body of Knowledge." Then, students ask, "Where do I find that book?" Well, it is not a book at all! It's the universe of literature that PMI® thinks is relevant for project management. So, it could encompass anything that is sold or referenced on the www.pmi.org website—any of the books or any of the magazine articles that are referenced there. We could spend more than a year studying and reading these books, and we would still have only made a small dent in this universe of literature on project management. Therefore, most students take a one-week intensive, PMP® Prep boot camp class to get all the essential information they need to prepare for the test.[2]

The *PMBOK® Guide* is only a guide or high-level framework for this *PMBOK.* (In effect, the *PMBOK® Guide* is the "Monarch Notes" or cheat-sheets to the *PMBOK!*) Also, it is well known that the *PMBOK® Guide* is a very difficult read. It is very abstract and cryptic, and most students find it to be one of the most boring books they've ever read! I tell my students that my "value-add" for them as an instructor is to be their interpreter of the *PMBOK® Guide.* I will read in-between the lines and explain what was really meant in many of these cryptic passages; I will explain why they included certain ITTO (inputs, tools–techniques, and outputs) for different processes; and I will provide good, concrete examples that will bring these abstract processes to life and make them more clear.

The reason the *PMBOK® Guide* is so cryptic and abstract is that it is not intended to be a specific methodology for how to do projects. Instead, it is intended to be a "framework" that supports all methodologies in all industries and for all contract types. It is intended to support the most

---

[2] In December 2019, PMI® announced that the PMP® Exam will be changing in very significant ways starting on July 1, 2020. They've said that 50 percent of the test questions will change, that 50 percent of the questions will now be based on Agile and Hybrid concepts, and they have also provided a list of 10 reference books that students should become acquainted with before taking the test. The 10 reference books include the *PMBOK® Guide,* the *Agile Practice Guide®*, plus another eight books. The total number of pages of all 10 books is 5,384! Later, in March 2020, because of the COVID-19 virus, the rollout of the new test was delayed until January 2, 2021.

complex projects. That is why this book is so abstract and generalized! It is supposed to be a framework that supports Agile methodologies as well as waterfall/predictive planning approaches. Yet, the *PMBOK® Guide* is more than 750 pages and is also accompanied by the *Agile Practice Guide®*, which is 167 pages! So, we have more than 900 pages for something that's supposed to be a framework! To put things in perspective, the draft of Version One that I worked with in 1994 to prepare for the PMP® exam was 64 pages. Version One (1996) was 176 pages.

Table 3.1 details the history and expansion of the *PMBOK® Guide* since its beginning in 1987. (Actually, the *PMBOK* released in 1987 was not called the *PMBOK® Guide!* It was actually called the "PMBOK"—Project Management Body of Knowledge.) PMI® later thought better of this, since no one book could be the complete "Body of Knowledge." Therefore, after 1987, all the versions have been "A Guide to the Project Management Body of Knowledge" or "*PMBOK® Guide.*"

Table 3.1 History of PMBOK® Guide Releases from 1987 though 2017

PMBOK® Guide Version	Date Released	Number of Pages	Number of KAs	Number of processes	Number of ITTO
Project Management Body of Knowledge (PMBOK)	March 28, 1987	80	8		
PMBOK® Guide-Draft Version one	August-1994	64	9	37	318
Version One	1996	176	9	37	359
Version Two (2000 version)	2000	211	9	39	
Version Three	December-2004	390	9	44	592
Version Four	December-2008	467	9	42	517
Version Five	December-2013	589	10	47	619
Version Six	September-2017	756	10	49	662/ (1418 w/ bullets!)

In Version Six, today, if you count all the bulleted items that are included in many tools–techniques, such as *Data Gathering, Data Representation, Data Analysis, Interpersonal and Team Skills*, and also include the bullets that support a number of key inputs (the Project Management Plan and "Project documents"), you have a staggering 1,400+ ITTO. Is this fundamental, core project knowledge? Is this something that adds to a "framework" for doing project management and applies to all projects? I think not. A small fraction of this ITTO is something that is used on a regular basis by PMs today. This does not make up a core foundation or framework for practicing PMs.

Very few practicing PMs regularly consult the *PMBOK® Guide* to see what tools–techniques should be used in a particular process or what other ITTO is relevant. We don't need to know whether a particular tool–technique (affinity diagrams) is a "data gathering" tool or a "data representation" tool. This is not core, fundamental project management knowledge that needs to be part of a framework. No practicing PM is going to have as part of their day-to-day tool kit an understanding of "bubble charts" or "influence diagrams" or "Monte Carlo simulation." They may remember a little bit at a high level about such tools–techniques, but if there is a special case where they think the tool–technique might have some application, they'll look up the tool on the Internet, or in other references, and find out what they need.

So, the *PMBOK® Guide* is filled with extraneous, nonessential information that is not really part of a framework for project management. I'm very sure that a high percentage of PMP® Prep instructors start their classes by warning the students that the *PMBOK® Guide* has nothing whatsoever to do with the "real world," and to successfully pass the PMP® exam, the students must completely forget about the real world. One of the worst strategies students could use for answering the tricky, situational questions is to ask themselves, "How would we solve this problem at our company and in our world." PMI® should be very taken aback by such statements.

In graduate school, as a teaching assistant for undergraduate logic classes, we would classify some arguments for positions as being "too strong." The argument included a lot of nonessential, nongermane information. The *PMBOK® Guide* is "too strong."

However, the *PMBOK® Guide* is also "too weak." It is missing key, core fundamental knowledge that should be part of the tool-kit of all PMs. Likewise, the *Agile Practice Guide®* leaves out essential concepts and topics that all PMs should know regarding Agile. For example, they don't discuss the different Agile estimating methods nor how these are used in different stages of the Agile lifecycle. This is important! This should be part of the *Agile Practice Guide®* as well as part of the *PMBOK® Guide.* We will touch on these estimating methods elsewhere in this chapter.

The two most important methodologies for managing projects today are (1) the traditional approach: waterfall, predictive planning, and EVM; and (2) Agile. Neither the *PMBOK® Guide* nor the *Agile Practice Guide®* provides much guidance at all about how and why one methodology is more appropriate in some places, and not in others. No case examples are provided. Of course, in this book, our most important goal was to discuss this as well as how hybrid approaches can be used.

In Version Six, PMI® has finally included Agile concepts to a much greater extent (in Version Five, Agile was only mentioned seven times), and they have even added on a companion document, the *Agile Practice Guide®*. They collaborated with the Agile Alliance in producing this 167-page book, but I don't believe they have gone far enough with including Agile concepts. They do not explain why Lean and Agile are crucial methodologies for all PMs to know about in our modern project world. The focus of Chapter 1 of this book is to try to make the case for why PMs need to know about both methodologies, and why hybrid project management is a necessity.

Key Items Missing from the PMBOK® Guide

Agile Concepts (Discussed in This Chapter)

- Agile estimating methods: T-shirt sizing, affinity estimating, planning poker, using "velocity" to map relative estimates to actual duration estimates
- Prioritization techniques: MoSCoW, Kano analysis, Monopoly money, 100-point method, "Prune the product tree."

Relevancy

- Shouldn't anything relevant for the PMI-ACP® (PMI Agile Certified Professional) exam also be relevant for the PMP® exam, and included in the *PMBOK® Guide*?
- Shouldn't anything relevant for the PMI-RMP (PMI Risk Management Professional) exam be relevant for the PMP® exam and, therefore, included in the *PMBOK® Guide*?
- I would argue, yes, the PMP® certification should be a superset, and include anything that is included in these other certifications too.

Terms/Concepts

- Traditional PM terms and concepts that have been deleted from Version Six, but were included in earlier versions.

Terms/Concepts	Definition
Delphi technique	Find ways to solicit the opinions, anonymously or in such a manner that the individuals being polled are not being influenced by the other team members
PERT (Program Evaluation and Review Technique)	Statistical tool designed to analyze and represent tasks involved in completing a given project
CCM (Critical Chain Method)	Had been a key tool–technique in *Develop Schedule* since Version Two

Suppose a young PM has just earned her CAPM® certification (Certified Associate in Project Management) and, in doing so, has read the *PMBOK® Guide* cover to cover and has thoroughly digested all 756 pages! If this young PM wanted to use all this knowledge as the basis for initiating, planning, executing, monitoring and controlling, and closing a new project, I think she would quickly give up in frustration! We would likely hear her say, "I don't have time to use all these processes and use all this ITTO! I hardly know where to begin!" … "I can't possibly create and update such a Project Management Plan with all 18 component pieces, and additionally update and maintain over 30 project documents!"

... "We will never get any work done!" ... "This would be completely impractical." We have to remember that the *PMBOK® Guide* is intended to support the most complex of projects, and in that world, perhaps the PM team is using most, if not all, of the 49 processes, and many of the ITTO. But the PM is not creating and updating all these plans and documents herself! She is delegating most of this documentation work to her team members, and she probably has a project management team of more than 10 people.

On the other hand, people find Agile very refreshing, because it is simpler and very easy to start using—especially Scrum. Scrum is the most popular of all the different Agile methodologies, and the practitioners say it is quite easy to adopt. Scrum does define a methodology of how to do a project and the Scrum advocates would say furthermore, "IT WORKS!" However, these same authors (e.g., Jeff Sutherland, Ken Schwaber, Mike Griffiths) also warn us that we should stick with Scrum for at least nine months before we start modifying any of the roles, meetings, or processes. They say Scrum is very easy to begin using, but is hard to perfect. Unfortunately, there are too many people who think they are doing Agile or Scrum, but are not!

Again, the *PMBOK® Guide* is not meant to be a methodology of how to do a project. Being an old software guy, I joke sometimes in my PMP® Prep classes that if the *PMBOK® Guide* were code, it would not compile. There are places where there is circular logic with the inputs and outputs of processes. For example, for the process *Estimate Costs,* "Resource Requirements" are a key input and "Cost Estimates" are the key output. However, for *Estimate Activity Resources,* "Cost Estimates" are a key input and the key output is "Resource Requirements." This is clearly circular, and things can't happen exactly this way. When I'm reviewing and explaining these processes in my classes, I just say that we need to give PMI® a pass on this circularity. We understand they are being somewhat "elliptical" in their description of the interaction of these processes. They really mean that we are often doing these two processes together and in parallel. We're doing a little bit of one, then some of the other, then coming back to the first process again, and so on. So, in reality, our handling of the processes is often circular. When students ask, "But what is the right sequence or flow of these processes?" the answer is, "It depends!"

It depends on the complexity of the project, the contract type, and, in general, what the team is trying to accomplish. There isn't one exact flow to the processes and many things are happening in parallel. I ask students in the PMP® Prep classes to imagine they are an Iron Chef in one of the contests on the Food Network channel. They have many things cooking on different stoves and baking in different ovens all at the same time, and they have a number of Sous-chefs working for them (members of the project management team).

In the Version Six *PMBOK® Guide,* a number of graphics depict the interaction of processes with one another. These drawings, such as the graphic for *Control Procurements* (found on page 493), show plans or documents coming from external processes. For example, the Project Management Plan—which is an output of *Develop Project Management Plan*—sends *Control Procurements* these items:

- Requirements documentation
- Risk Management Plan
- Procurement Management Plan
- Change Management Plan
- Schedule Baseline

They also show inputs coming into the process from *Project documents, Integrated Change Control, Direct and Manage Project Work, Plan Procurement Management, Conduct Procurements, and the Enterprise/Organization.*

Similarly, they show the outputs of the process (*Closed Procurements, Work Performance Information, Change Requests, ...*) and then show processes where these are inputs, and plans (e.g., the Project Management Plan) which are updated with this information.

However, this is not a perfect flowchart of the logical connections between ITTO and the various processes. In the *PMBOK® Guide*, there are numerous passages where they say

> these processes are presented as discrete processes with defined interfaces, while in practice they overlap and interact in ways that cannot be completely detailed in the *PMBOK® Guide. These*

processes interact with each other and with processes in other Knowledge Areas.[3]

There are some PMP® Prep books that teach that there is one exact flowchart to these processes. But this is not correct, and they are leading their readers astray! Remember that on an Agile project, we are using all phases in each iteration, and it should go without saying that all Process Groups are being used in each iteration, too.[4] Furthermore, it's up to the team to choose what they will work on next, the sequencing of the processes, and what the process flow will be.

Even if we're using a waterfall, sequential flow for the project and using predictive planning (complete all the "planning phases" first before starting the "execution" phases), there will still be some back and forth between planning processes. We may complete the scope planning processes and start the schedule planning processes, but when we get to *Develop Schedule*, we realize the project will take too long, and we will

---

[3] See the last sentence at the bottom of page 129 in the Version Six *PMBOK® Guide* for Chapter 5 on Project Scope Management Chapter.

[4] At an even more detailed level, many people, even PMPs, misunderstand the relationship between process groups and phases. PMI® emphatically states in the *PMBOK® Guide* that "Process Groups are not phases!" They used to put this in bold print, but in Version Six of the *PMBOK® Guide*, this is still emphasized in four different places. (See page 18 for one such instance.) Instead, process groups are used inside phases, and if we are really worthy of the PMP® certification, we will use processes from all five process groups in each phase! Just like the project overall, each phase must be authorized and initiated; similarly, each phase must be formally closed; we will execute in every phase because we are creating deliverables in every phase; if we are executing, we are necessarily monitoring and controlling (but monitoring and controlling checks on all four of the other process groups). We are always asking from beginning to end, "Are we on schedule?" ... "Are we on budget?" ... "Are we meeting Quality requirements?" ... And so on. It's hard to see why we would need to do planning out toward the end of the project, but if we are good, we will be doing that also! If for no other reason, we're always looking for ways to make improvements. Do Kaizen! Doing continuous improvement will require planning, so we could be doing planning even at the end of the project. Also, we may purposefully wait until the end of the project to plan the "punch list," for example.

miss a key schedule constraint. So, we go back to *Define Scope* and eliminate some requirements from the scope statement, so we can meet the schedule constraint. Or, we proceed into the cost planning processes, and we realize the project, as-is, will exceed a key budget constraint. So, again, we go back and eliminate some requirements that weren't high priority, or we find different resources that are less expensive, or we find a different engineering design solution that is less expensive, but will meet the functional requirements.

I often hear, during PMIWDC dinner meetings, comments from PMs such as, "Yes, we're required to follow the processes as defined in the *PMBOK® Guide*." I don't comment, but I'm thinking that is not possible, really (because there is no one exact process flow), and it's not advisable to try to use the *PMBOK® Guide* in this way!

Yet, there is a lot of core, sound knowledge in the *PMBOK® Guide* that all PMs should learn about and pay attention to. Even in 1995, when I was preparing for the PMP® exam, I found the amount of material that was covered for the exam to be quite overwhelming. The types of projects I was managing involved only a subset of all the processes in the nine Knowledge Areas (KAs) of the time, and I only used a small subset of the tools and techniques for the processes. There were topics and concepts in a number of the KAs I had never heard about. For example, cost-reimbursable contracts were not something that I had had experience with; I only worked on projects being executed under a fixed price contract. In the early 1990s, we had our own internal Total Quality Management (TQM) methodology, and I had not heard much at all about Six Sigma or ISO-9000. I was not using EVM on any of my projects and a number of the topics and concepts in the Time Management and the Risk Management KA were new to me. So, I found it to be quite eye opening to get exposure to such topics as these and others that were needed for the PMP® exam. This was a good thing! I think most students in my PMP® classes feel the same way, today. I thought it would be quite challenging and even refreshing if I were assigned to a project where we did need to address a much larger set of the processes and concepts in all KAs of the *PMBOK® Guide.*

Important Concepts in the *PMBOK® Guide*, Ways Agile Expands upon These Concepts, and Places Where Agile Is Not a Good Fit

In Chapter 1, I explained what I think are three of the most important KAs in the *PMBOK® Guide*: *Scope Management, Communications Management, and Stakeholder Management.* We've also touched on the three key types of contracts, how fixed price contracts can be used with Agile, and how Agile expands on the T&M contract types.

I won't repeat that entire discussion again, but the bottom line is that project management is a very difficult job, no doubt about it! It's very difficult, because our job entails getting all the different stakeholders on the project—with all their different needs, different wants, and inconsistent requirements—onto "the same page." We must have a well-written scope statement and very well written (SMART) acceptance criteria for all our deliverables. The scope statement must define boundaries and exclusions that tell the stakeholders what is in scope and what is not. This is very difficult to do, because on many of our projects, no matter how powerful we are, many of the stakeholders will outrank us. Getting everyone onto the same page is going to tax the limits of our capabilities of using negotiation skills, communication skills, and influencing skills. But if we are not successful in achieving this goal, the project is surely going to fail, and it's going to be the PM that takes the blame. At some point in time, almost all PMs are going to be involved in a complex project with difficult stakeholders, and it's going to be essential to create that detailed scope statement that is much like a very detailed SOW in a fixed price contract where all the I's are dotted and the T's are crossed, and there is no room for confusion about what was called for in our deliverables.

Yet, we went further and explained there will be situations where we can achieve all these goals (have a very well written scope statement with boundaries, exclusions, and SMART acceptance criteria for the deliverables), and we can still fail! How can that be? Well, it might take us a year or two to create the deliverables called for in the scope statement, and by the time we delivered these products or services to the customer, it might be clear that they were no longer of value. We could meet the scope statement explicitly, we could be on budget, and we could be on schedule, but we could still fail! We could meet the terms of the contract with the customer, so we are going to get paid, but we really didn't achieve value, and therefore, we were not successful. The world had changed in the two years it took us to create these deliverables, and they no longer had the value that was first envisioned. The customer will probably not use our company to manage their next project and will probably not provide a recommendation for our services!

We then explained that using Agile and Lean addresses this very real problem in our modern world. We will interact with the customer and the product owner on a much more frequent basis than we did in the traditional model, we are grooming the value chain using Lean, and we will create tangible, empirical results in very short iterations. This helps us ensure we are creating value and provides our sponsor and other senior managers empirical data for doing the "kill points," so they can shut down projects that are not creating value.

The four planning processes in Scope Management in the *PMBOK® Guide* are

- *Plan Scope Management*
- *Collect Requirements*
- *Define Scope*
- *Create WBS*

There are key tools–techniques defined for each of these planning steps in the *PMBOK® Guide*. But I believe that PMI® would have been better off by also adding key tools–techniques from the Agile methodologies. The theme in *Collect Requirements* is to err on the side of inclusiveness, touch base with as many stakeholders as possible from the Stakeholder Register, and make sure we haven't missed or misunderstood any requirements. Key tools–techniques mentioned in the Version Six *PMBOK® Guide* are listed in the following table:

Key Tools–Techniques	Description
Brainstorming (pp. 78, 80, 85, ...)	Create an environment where everyone is encouraged to participate. (Use small groups, where everyone feels free to participate.) No bad ideas! Encourage creativity
Mind-mapping (pp. 144, 284, 521, 711)	Create a "mind map" of the solution with all its features. Get very graphical and include imagery of the solution. Also, get very colorful. As you hierarchically decompose the solution, build out different neural paths for these parts of the solution
Affinity diagrams (pp. 144, 293, 698)	As the team is brainstorming ideas, have them write down their ideas on Post-it notes, and then paste these Post-it notes to the walls of the room where the meeting is being held. Then, have the team rearrange all the Post-it notes to put ideas that have commonality or affinity close to each other
Nominal Group Technique (pp. 144–145, 712)	Again, first brainstorm in small groups to generate a lot of ideas. Then, have the group (or a different group) review these ideas to rank them and sort them
QFD (Quality Function Deployment)—(p. 145)	This is a favorite tool–technique of Six Sigma and other proprietary quality methodologies and used in manufacturing and engineering. The idea is very simple: Get your engineers out of their office and have them go meet with the customers to have productive conversations, so the engineers can truly understand what the customers are looking for in the products. QFD uses "Voice of the Customer" in this process. Matrix diagrams and the "House of Quality" are also part of this process. We are mapping the customer's requirements onto the engineering requirements in a "matrix diagram," and this matrix often resembles a house, hence, "the House of Quality"
JAD (Joint Application Design)—(p. 145)	Very similar to QFD, but is used in the software industry. Get those systems analysts and software engineers out of their office and into productive meetings with the customer to truly understand what the customer is asking for in this software application. Don't assume we know what the customer wants! Just because a feature is "state-of-the-art," don't assume it's something that the customer is requesting. Instead get out of our office, meet with the customers, and follow them around in their daily work day to see what they truly need. Even better: try out their job for part of the day!
Prototyping (pp. 147, 717)	As quickly as we can, in short iterations, create models or prototypes of what the customer is requesting. As we mentioned earlier, think of Doug DeCarlo's quote: "if a picture is worth a thousand words, a prototype is worth a thousand pictures!" In Agile, the prototypes that are being created in each iteration are not throwaway prototypes or models. They are just a subset of the features and requirements the customer is requesting, but they are something that can go into production

However, Agile methodologies include a number of interesting and creative tools–techniques that could enhance and expand on this effort:

Key Tools–Techniques	Description
Quiet writing	The team members are given five to seven minutes to individually write down their ideas. Then the ideas are shared and reviewed with the group. This minimizes "anchoring" or members influencing each other in generating the ideas
Round robin	A token is passed around the group. Each member gets a turn to offer an idea and then pass the token to the next member, who can add thoughts or build on the previous idea
Remember the future	We ask the entire team (sponsor, development team, users, ...) to imagine how the product/service will look several weeks after the release has ended • Spend 20 minutes where each team member writes down their ideas, individually, on sticky notes (Post-it notes) • Place the notes around the room on the walls • Spend 20 minutes ± where the team reviews the notes, removes duplicates, and rearranges the notes according to commonality/affinity (affinity diagram)

As we said earlier, *Collect Requirements* was all about erring on the side of inclusiveness and capturing as many requirements as possible. Since it is very common for there to be inconsistencies between the requirements that the different stakeholders want in the project, an essential point of the next planning process—*Define Scope*—is to resolve these inconsistencies and incompatibilities by defining boundaries and exclusions. The key tools–techniques provided in the *PMBOK® Guide* in *Define Scope* are *Product Analysis* and *Alternatives Analysis.* "Product Analysis" in manufacturing or engineering identifies "how can I achieve the required functionality for the least cost." Product Analysis in software is simply Systems Analysis or Systems Engineering.

However, something key is missing in what is provided to us in the *PMBOK® Guide*! This missing ingredient is provided by Lean and is a key part of the numerous Agile methodologies: this is "Prioritization." I think the different Prioritization techniques mentioned in various Agile methodologies should really be a part of *Define Scope.* These Prioritization techniques include:

- MoSCoW (M: must have; S: should have; C: could have; W: won't have)
- Kano analysis
- Prune the product tree

These Prioritization techniques will help us determine what are the 20 percent highest priority requirements that will provide 80 percent of the customer's need.

Using the MoSCoW analysis (or "*MoSCoW*" where the capitalized and underlined letters indicate levels of priority), the team determines which requirements are required:

Priority	Desired Requirements
One	Must Have requirements—there's no point in going forward without these
Two	Should Have requirements—we also really want to have these, if at all possible
Three	Could Have (or, would like to have) requirements
Four	Won't Have requirements—for the time being, we don't see including these requirements

Kano analysis is another excellent Prioritization technique used in the Agile methodologies. We should look deeper into features, requirements, and preferences. We should classify preferences into four different ways:

Preferences Classification	Feature Attribute
Delighter or Exciter	Unexpected or novel features that yield high levels of customer satisfaction
Satisfier	Features that bring value: the more, the better
Dissatisfier	Expected basic features that, if missing, will cause customer dissatisfaction. However, their presence doesn't increase customer satisfaction
Indifferent	Features that have no impact on the customer one way or another; therefore, since there is no impact from these, they should be eliminated

Some other very easy-to-use Prioritization schemes in Agile are:

Prioritization Scheme	Scheme Details
Monopoly money	Each team member is given a specified amount of monopoly money (perhaps $500) to spread around between the different features and requirements in the backlog as they see fit. The features or backlog items that end up with the most money have the highest priority
100-point method	Similar to monopoly money, each team member is given 100 points to spread around between the different backlog items as they see fit
Dot voting	Each team member is given a number of dots to spread around between the backlog items as they see fit

In summary for *Define Scope*, the *PMBOK® Guide* correctly emphasizes the need for the scope statement to define boundaries and exclusions and "to get everyone onto the same page." As we emphasized earlier, this can be very hard to do, and I think this is the essence of the hard part of project management. It is just very natural for customers, the sponsor, and the product owner to want everything under the sun included in the project for requirements (the product backlog). Furthermore, at the start of the project they think of everything as essential or priority one! It's going to tax all our best soft skills, negotiation skills, and other people skills to force these different stakeholders to do prioritization. This is not something that is currently included as a tool–technique for *Define Scope* in the *PMBOK® Guide*, though it should be. Agile brings to the table some very interesting and creative ways to help a team do prioritization.

Create WBS is the fourth and the last of the planning processes in Scope Management. The key output of *Create WBS* is our first baseline: the *scope baseline*. The scope baseline is a little unusual and different from the other three baselines in that it has three parts: *scope statement, WBS, and WBS dictionary*. For the traditionalists, the WBS is absolutely critical and drives all other planning for the project. It is the "cornerstone" of planning for the project. What is the origin and source of the WBS? Earned Value Analysis! And we know that EV comes to us from DoD in the 1960s. The EV practitioners and traditionalists would say that it is unthinkable to manage a project without having a WBS. Again, this drives all other planning: it will drive scheduling, cost estimating, and budgeting, as well as figuring out quality, risks, and what you want to outsource in your project. The "100 percent rule" is "If it's not in the WBS, it's not in the project!"

However, in Agile, we don't use a WBS! Are the Agilists making a huge mistake? Actually, the Agilists rely on something quite similar to a WBS—it is a hierarchical decomposition of all the requirements and features of the project, but they call this structure an "FBS" (feature breakdown structure). On one side, the WBS is all about nouns or things. It is a hierarchical structure where we're decomposing things like products; decomposing the products into parts; then, parts into components; then, components down to subassemblies; and so on. The WBS also needs to include "project scope," which will be plans, documents, blueprints, and such, but these are still nouns (documents).

The FBS, on the other hand, is comprised of features and stories, and these are all about customer-facing value. The template for a story is

> "As a <Role>, I want <Functionality>, so that <Business benefit>."
> Answers: "Who is asking for this?" Also, "Why are we doing this?

This same template applies to features and epics, as well as stories.[5]

Is the distinction we are defining, here, between work-packages and stories or the WBS and the FBS something quite minor and cosmetic? No, it is not. It is actually something that points out a key aspect of Agile.

---

[5] The *Agile Practice Guide*® does a poor job of defining stories/features/epics and differentiating between stories and WBS elements! They only define "Stories" in the glossary in one sentence: "A User Story is a brief description of deliverable valuable for a specific user." Someone could easily misread this as another term for a deliverable. Instead, stories are all about something that has customer-facing value. They are about functional capabilities for the customer, not about a specific engineering design. At the lowest level in the WBS (work-packages), we are often dealing with an engineering component: parts, components of parts, subassemblies, and so on.

In the classic traditional way of doing project management, the PM is accountable for the Project Management Plan and all 18 of its component pieces. Once this formal written plan has been approved, the PM starts handing out sections of the Project Management Plan to the different team members to implement. But the work-packages are specified in detail in the WBS, so it is clear exactly what the team members should be creating. In Agile, things are quite different. The stories or features define fairly high-level functional requirements that the product owner wants created, and there might be a number of different engineering approaches for achieving that required functionality. During an iteration in the Agile project, a lot of freedom and trust is provided to the team members to determine, on their own, the best way to implement the required functionality. The features and stories are not defining detailed engineering specifications as you would find for many work-packages.

Also, the Agilists do not speak of baselines. Perhaps this is because they are much more accepting of change, and they are expecting significant change from iteration-to-iteration. The *PMBOK® Guide* allows that the baselines may be changed over time during the project (we may do "re-baselining"), but I believe the expectation for the traditionalists would be that this change will be much less frequent and more measured. In some of the original textbooks for project management, such as Harold Kerzner's book, *Project Management—A Systems Approach to Planning, Scheduling, and Controlling*, he says scope changes should be kept to a minimum.

People not only confuse stories and features with work-packages or other WBS elements, there is also quite a bit of confusion in the real world about other Agile terms. Many traditionalists think the Agile community has just redefined many traditional terms and concepts and given them new names. DAU (Defense Acquisition University) has even published a white paper mapping the Agile terms onto the traditional terms. This mapping is incorrect on numerous counts! The *Agile Practice Guide®* should address this point and clear up these errors. Here are essential points in the DAU white paper (Table 3.2):

Table 3.2 DAU —Mapping traditional WBS terminology to Agile

Agile Term	Traditional (WBS) Reference	Comments and Objections to the Mapping
Product Backlog	Entire scope of the project	All the approved requirements for the project. All the capabilities or epics which can be hierarchically decomposed into features which can be further decomposed into stories. Includes both functional requirements and non-functional requirements: (e.g., supporting IT architecture, network requirements, security requirements, ... for an application being created). This mapping is acceptable
Iteration	Phase	In Agile, we divide the project into "time-boxed" iterations which are one to four weeks each. An "increment" of the product backlog is created in each iteration or Sprint, and this maps well to the idea that in each phase a deliverable is created. Objection: In the "development iterations" all of the classic phases are used. We will do planning, executing, testing, and gaining acceptance in each development iteration
Release	Project	A Release is the number of iterations needed to create useful functionality for the customer. This mapping is acceptable
Product Roadmap	Schedule	Shows the timing: How many iterations will the project take? Choose the iterations in a release when features/stories will be created. Objection: Agilists don't track the schedule with a scheduling tool such as MSProject or Primavera. They don't speak of the critical path. They think the effort to do predictive planning, and put together a schedule for things occurring 6 months or farther into the future is a mistake.
Epic/ Capability	WBS element at or above the Control Account Level	High-level requirement. Objection: Again, epics, features, and stories are all about customer facing value. Many nodes and elements in a WBS are about actual engineering design elements
Feature	Work-packages perhaps?—Next level below the Control Account Level	Epics are decomposed into features. Objection: Again, epics, features, and stories are all about customer facing value. Many nodes and elements in a WBS are about actual engineering design elements
Stories	Activities—next level below features	Features are decomposed into stories. Objection: Again, epics, features, and stories are all about customer facing value. Many nodes and elements in a WBS are about actual engineering design elements

Key Lessons in Other Knowledge Areas in the *PMBOK® Guide*

Integration Management

Integration Management is a key KA. I think students in my PMP® Prep classes are often surprised when I say we can make a very good case that *Integration Management* is the most important of all the 10 KAs. (Actually, when I get into the next KA, Scope Management, I qualify the previous statement and say that *Integration Management and Scope Management* are tied for first place.) Why is *Integration Management* so important? Because this typifies for PMI® what we do as PMs: We are integrators. We are integrating all the different plans together. It is not our job to develop all the individual pieces (18 component pieces!) of the Project Management Plan nor even all the different work-packages and components of the WBS. We don't have time to do that for a large, complex project, and we are not the right people for doing this type of detailed planning. So, we're delegating much of this planning work to our team members and other specialists on the project. Our role is to be accountable for the entire plan: to ensure nothing is missing, everything is consistent and balanced, and priorities are properly maintained.

It's the same thing for executing. For a large, complex construction project, perhaps one that is taking place over 25 square miles, we cannot be in all places at the same time directing the execution of work. We're delegating the supervision of this work to other project management team members. Of course, the same point applies to monitoring and controlling. Again, we cannot be in all places at the same time, so we're delegating measuring progress to other team members and also measuring our performance against the baselines to determine what variance exists. Again, the PM is accountable for ensuring all this execution and monitoring and controlling work is occurring properly, and everything is consistent and integrated.

A metaphor that is often used for describing the role of the PM is that we are the conductor of the project orchestra. We are ensuring that all the sections of the orchestra are in tune, that everyone is playing their part at the right time, that the brass section isn't drowning out the woodwinds (that everything is balanced), and the moments of crescendo and moments of pianissimo in the symphony are properly emphasized. But what we do will involve much more than that! Our project is not about just directing a specific performance of a concert. No; we are often planning out a whole series of concerts: picking the right venue, choosing the right orchestra, choosing the composer (Will we choose Dvorak, Mahler, Beethoven, Mozart, or Rachmaninoff?). How will we do the advertising and the marketing? Oftentimes, our project is going to address all of these types of things that involve work in all 10 KAs and all 5 Process Groups. Our goal will be to ensure proper integration across all these KAs and across the Process Groups.

In Version Six of the *PMBOK® Guide*, PMI® is emphasizing that PMs must be much more than just effective managers: we must also be leaders! In Version Six they give us a very good slide on page 64 that depicts the differences between being an effective manager and being an effective leader. They provide a table of characteristics of managers and then contrast these with characteristics of good, effective leaders.

The mapping of some of the key contrasting characteristics goes like this:

Characteristics of Managers	***Characteristics of Effective Leaders***
Focus on administration	Focus on innovation
Use positional power	Guide and influence with relational power
Rely on control	Inspire trust
Focus on near-term goals	Focus on long-term vision
Focus on the bottom line	Focus on the horizon
Accept status quo	Challenge the status quo
Focus on how and when	Focus on what and why
Focus on doing things right	Focus on doing the right things

We've all worked for people in our past who were very effective and successful managers, who insured the team successfully completed the work that was called for in the contract or SOW or the Project Management Plan, but they didn't really inspire us or excite us or sell the vision for the project. "Why are we really doing this?" ... "What is the value that we are creating?" What PMI® has outlined in the slide above is that leaders do inspire the team and do sell the "Vision." As Simon Sinek describes in his book, *Start with Why*, to be truly successful, we must also focus on "Why." Sinek says in this book that successful companies and successful leaders always address "Why" and inspire their employees and team members with the vision for the company (or the project). The most successful companies inspire their customers with the "Vision" or "Why."

How does this all align with the Agile view of the PM? Well, in Agile, we do not have the classic PM as defined in the *PMBOK® Guide.* No; the closest thing to a PM on an Agile project is the Scrum Master or the Coach, and the Scrum Master (or Coach) is not the accountable and empowered integrator as defined in the *PMBOK® Guide.* The Scrum Master is a "Servant Leader." Their role is primarily to help the team members ensure they are not interfered with during the iteration or the Sprint and be the caretakers of the Agile methodology. (If there are questions about how to use the Scrum methodology—how to run the different meetings or what the roles on the project really entail—they are the person or resource to go to for the answers.) This Scrum Master is not accountable for the project management plan and is not handing out the different pieces of the plan to the team members and managing the execution against the plan, or monitoring and controlling progress. No, the team members themselves are the ones accountable for the plan, are choosing what stories will be worked on next, and are accountable for what is created in the iteration.

How can that work? Don't we need a single point of contact? The "One throat to choke!" so to speak? The person that is accountable for the project? How can a team be accountable for anything? Management is going to want that single point of contact, aren't they? Many senior PMs who are PMP®s and first introduced to Agile are quite confused by this whole concept of no PM, and even threatened. They are either thinking to themselves or asking out loud, "Isn't this type of project manager really just a 'Coordinator' (as defined in a Weak Matrix organization in the *PMBOK® Guide*) with very reduced authority?"—"What company is going to pay me my current salary as a senior PMP® project manager when I'm just this type of coordinator?"—"I'm not liking this at all!"

But the Agilists will point out that we can make this type of concept work (along with the reduced authority of the Scrum Master), because we are doing our project in very short iterations and bringing in the product owner and other managers on a very frequent basis (at minimum, every one to four weeks) to review and accept what the team has created during the iteration. Management can wait the one to four weeks to see what the team has created. They are agreeing not to interfere with, or interrupt, the team during the iteration. If they have objections to what the team created during the iteration (the product increment) then the team will take accountability for the problems and will change the backlog items for the next Sprint or iteration.

Even though I agree that this concept of the Scrum Master as servant leader can work, I believe that on large, complex projects, the *PMBOK® Guide* description of the role of the PM is often needed. For a large, complex project, I think we do need a single point of accountability, and we do need someone who will take on the leadership role. Who is this person going to be? I don't know of many product owners, perhaps former business development people, who want to take on this much of an expanded role. They already have enough on their plates as business analysts or business developers.

So, I think there is a disconnect and a gap between what is described in the *PMBOK® Guide* for the role of the PM and what is defined in the Agile literature as the role for the Scrum Master or Coach. The role of the product owner is also not addressed in the *PMBOK® Guide.* These disconnects need to be addressed by both PMI® and the Agile community, especially for large, complex projects. As we said before, we might need more than just one product owner. Also, more discussion is required as to what the career path is for becoming a successful product owner. Are these people typically former or existing business development people? Are they former PMs taking on additional responsibility? On a large, complex project, getting everyone onto the same page is a very difficult job—as we described—and we can't gloss over this just by thinking that designating a single product owner will easily solve these problems.

Quality Management

Quality Management is another key KA, and I think there are important themes and concepts for all PMs that are addressed here. What is the definition of quality for PMI®? In the *PMBOK® Guide*, PMI® decided to go with the ISO-9000 definition which is "Quality is the degree to which a set of inherent characteristics fulfill requirements." That is certainly a mouthful and is not very memorable! This ISO definition definitely leveraged Philip Crosby's definition and his definition was "Quality is conformance to requirements." That one is easier to deal with! But I like Joseph Juran's definition the best, "Quality is fitness for use." I think his definition strikes at a key point that quality is really about meeting customer satisfaction goals and providing value. We can build products that meet all the scope requirements, but fail quality, because they are not fit for use. We described a scenario in Chapter 1 that was an exact fit for this situation and which Agile addresses. If we are tasked with creating a new software application and we do predictive planning to exhaustively obtain all the requirements—both scope requirements and quality requirements—up front at the beginning of the project, but then take two years to develop this new application, in almost all cases, the new application will not meet the customer's needs and will not provide value. It will not be "fit for use." The world has changed. There will be better technologies and much better design approaches available, and this application that was designed two years earlier will no longer be a good solution. The new software application could meet all the scope requirements defined, but not meet the customers' quality requirements.

There are three processes in Quality Management: *Plan Quality Management*, *Manage Quality* (*or Perform Quality Assurance*), and *Control Quality.* Where did we originally obtain the quality requirements for the project? (Hint: It wasn't in any of these three processes!) Actually, we obtained the quality requirements in the Scope Management KA in the process, *Collect Requirements.* In *Collect Requirements*, we err on the side of inclusiveness. We touch base with all the stakeholders and stakeholder groups in the Stakeholder Register; we use JAD (Joint Application Design) and QFD (Quality Function Development); we get very creative and do mind-mapping and brainstorming to exhaustively discover all the product requirements, project requirements, all the scope requirements, and the quality requirements for this project. A subset of all these requirements will get formally approved in the next process, *Define Scope.* So, it follows that the scope statement addresses not only scope requirements, but also quality requirements. How is that? Where are the quality requirements in the scope statement? They are in the scope statement's acceptance criteria. In the process *Validate Scope*, where we bring in the customer to formally approve our deliverables, they are not going to approve these deliverables unless the deliverables meet both scope and quality. The customer will be inspecting the deliverables and comparing how they meet up against the acceptance criteria in the scope statement.

Quality Management is one of the few KAs where PMI® is borrowing a lot from operations management and proprietary methodologies outside of project management. These proprietary methodologies include Six Sigma, TQM, ISO-9000, Just in Time (JIT), the Toyota Production System (including Lean), and Capability Maturity Model Integration (CMMI). The Toyota Production System was developed in the early 1980s, but in 2003, Mary and Tom Poppendieck translated this for software and wrote *Lean Software Development*, which became part of the Agile movement. As I said before, Lean is a key part of all the different Agile methodologies.

A key part of all the mainstream proprietary quality methodologies is to be proactive and to prevent quality problems. The old-fashioned view for the right way to achieve quality was to test your products for quality defects and do inspection and testing very well. The modern view is to design quality into products and eliminate problems at the design stage.

Why are these operational proprietary methodologies that define the right ways to do quality assurance and quality control important for project management? Why did PMI® make this one of the core KAs in the *PMBOK® Guide*? The idea is fairly simple, I think. As we're doing our project, we should take a long-term view and protect our company going out into the operational part of the lifecycle. We should do "lifecycle costing," making sure the quality metrics and goals we are defining for our project protect the company even out into operations. The idea is to not make short-range decisions that save money in the project lifecycle, but avoid poor designing or low quality, which could cost the company much more money in the long term once into operations.

An important concept that is handled in both the Cost Chapter and the Quality Chapter in the *PMBOK® Guide* is "Cost of Quality" or COQ. This is also a key topic in many of the quality proprietary methodologies such as Six Sigma. COQ also overlaps the concept of doing lifecycle costing. As we are estimating our costs for the project, we should ensure we have built into these estimates all the things involved with achieving the right level of quality for products and services. COQ entails all the costs of achieving quality—the costs of succeeding at quality and doing things right as well as the costs if we fail. The costs of succeeding at quality are called "costs of conformance." The costs that are borne by the project if we fail to meet our quality metrics and goals are called "costs of nonconformance."

The costs of conformance can be broken into two subcategories: prevention costs and appraisal costs. Prevention costs are the cost of being proactive and preventing quality problems. Investing in prevention is the least expensive thing we can do to meet quality! This is investing in things like training your people; providing them with the right tools and equipment, so they can achieve high-quality products; allowing them enough time to create products with the right quality; and so on. Appraisal costs are the reactive costs of doing the tests and the inspections and maintaining all the different test equipment.

The nonconformance category also has two subcategories: internal failure costs and external failure costs. Internal failure costs are things we discover within the project team before the product gets shipped to the customer. Perhaps we discover a defect in one of our products in testing. As a result, we're going to have to do rework or defect repair and the item that failed the test might not be of any use to us at this point and, therefore, might become scrap inventory. These are examples of internal failure costs. External failure costs are the costs that hit the project if the customer discovers the problem. Examples of these types of costs are warranty replacements, lost business, loss of reputation, and liability costs. These costs can be huge! These costs could even cause the company to go out of business. (Liability costs, alone, could cause a company to go out of business.)

Figures 3.1 and 3.2 are slides summarizing the information on the different subcategories in COQ.

I. Cost of Conformance

A) Prevention Costs: - (The lowest cost of quality):
- ✓ Quality planning
- ✓ Quality training
- ✓ Providing time for the team to design for quality
- ✓ Obtaining right tools and equipment
- ✓ Document processes

B) Appraisal Costs:
- ✓ Testing - (includes destructive testing losses)
- ✓ Inspection
- ✓ Surveys
- ✓ Calibrating and maintaining test equipment

Figure 3.1 Cost of quality

II. Cost of Non-Conformance

A) Internal Failure Costs: - (Discovered by the project before the product is shipped):
- ✓ Scrap
- ✓ Rework (Repeat Service)
- ✓ High insurance costs
- ✓ Low team morale
- ✓ Excessive inspections
- ✓ Decreased efficiency

B) External Failure Costs: (The highest COQ sub-category. Costs discovered by the customer, after the product is shipped .)
- ✓ Warranty costs
- ✓ Lost business, lost customers
- ✓ Loss of reputation
- ✓ Negative press
- ✓ Liability costs

Figure 3.2 Cost of quality (continued)

In 1979, one of the early pioneers for quality, Philip Crosby, wrote the book *Quality Is Free.* But what could he have possibly meant by this? Sure, achieving high quality or the right level of quality is very important, but nothing is free, correct? What do you mean, Mr. Crosby? Crosby meant this: there is a huge ROI by investing in being proactive; all our investments in the *prevention* category in COQ will result in much lower costs in the nonconformance category (internal failure costs and external failure costs). The reductions in these subcategories in nonconformance will far outweigh the investment that was made in prevention, so that investment was free!

Lastly, another key concept discussed in the *PMBOK® Guide* and all the key quality methodologies is to use the plan-do-check-act (PDCA) loop to achieve continuous improvement, or do "Kaizen." As we said in Chapter 1, we should always strive to make small incremental improvements in all aspects of our project: our products, our services, our processes, and our plans and documents. We should use this PDCA loop provided to us by Deming and Shewhart to help achieve this goal. Don't try to solve everything at once. Don't try "to boil the whole ocean." Do a little bit of planning, execute against those plans, and then "check and act" to see how well you are doing. Then, go back and do more planning, executing, and testing to achieve continuous improvement. Doesn't this sound like Agile? Doesn't this sound like using very short iterations to groom the value chain? Yes, of course it does!

In what ways does Agile build on these important concepts and help us in achieving the right level of quality? In Agile, as we said in Chapter 1, we are speeding up the PDCA loop very significantly by increasing the frequency of feedback loops. (Remember the nested levels of feedback loops used on XP projects?) We are also significantly increasing the frequency of communications with our customer and other stakeholders. We are also demonstrating something empirical and tangible to them on a very frequent basis. This is very valuable. As Doug DeCarlo said, "If a picture is worth a thousand words, a prototype is worth a thousand pictures."

Estimating: Duration Estimates and Cost Estimates

There are four estimating methods that play an important part in the *PMBOK® Guide* in three of the KAs: *Schedule Management* (this was called *Time Management* in earlier versions of the *PMBOK® Guide*), *Cost Management*, and *Resource Management*. These four estimating methods are *Analogous Estimating, Bottom-Up Estimating, Parametric Estimating, and Three-Point Estimating*. (The three processes where they are featured as key tools–techniques are *Estimate Activity Durations*, *Estimate Costs*, and *Estimate Activity Resources*. In *Estimate Activity Resources*, only three of the estimating methods are featured: *Analogous Estimating*, *Bottom-Up Estimating*, and *Parametric Estimating*.)

For students preparing for the PMP® exam, we teach that *Bottom-Up Estimating* is the favorite estimating method, since it provides the most accurate estimates. On the downside, this type of estimate takes more time to create and, therefore, is more expensive. On a fairly typical project, we might have several thousand activities that make up the project (that are spread between several hundred work-packages). With *Bottom-Up Estimating*, the team is examining details of each activity to see what resources are needed—both tools and labor expertise. From below the activity level, they are creating an estimate. Then, in a bottom-up fashion, they are rolling this up from the activity level to the work-package level; then, to the control account level; and then, for the entire project. It will take the team days and days of time to create this type of estimate and will be quite expensive to create. However, if they do things this way, they will get their most accurate estimate. Also, we cannot do *Bottom-Up Estimating* until we are fairly far along with the different planning processes. We must have progressed far enough to be into the Time Management (Scheduling) processes, so that we have decomposed the work of the project down to the most detailed level: *Activities*.

If *Bottom-Up Estimating* is the most preferred type of estimating method, then *Analogous Estimating* is the least preferred. It is least preferred because it is least accurate. However, on the good side, Analogous Estimates are easy to create and don't cost much money. We can also do *Analogous Estimating* at the beginning of the project at a time when we haven't done any other planning. *Analogous Estimates* can also be called Top-Down estimates. In essence, at the top levels of the project (or in the top one or two levels in the WBS) we are comparing this project to an earlier project, and they appear to be very similar, very analogous. But what do we inevitably find out at a later time when we have progressed into more detailed levels of planning? Of course, once we get down to level IV or level V in the WBS, we often discover these projects were not so similar after all! Therefore, that original analogous estimate is not accurate at all. When we do our project with the waterfall approach, we often use analogous estimating to create the original high-level estimates that go into the Project Charter. These original estimates in the Charter—such as the initial budget estimate—oftentimes have the accuracy of a rough order of magnitude (ROM) estimate. For PMI®, the accuracy of a ROM can range between –25 and +75 percent. This means that when the real costs are learned, we learn the real costs could be 25 percent less than this ROM, or 75 percent more. So, the ROM was very "rangy." Nonetheless, this analogous estimate was very easy to create, did not take much time, and was not expensive to create.

Parametric Estimating is very useful when we are in the "cookie-cutter world," where we have done a type of project hundreds and hundreds of times before and we have very good historical records from previous projects from which we can build parametric models to get estimates of time and cost. Back in the days of third-generation language programming (using COBOL or Fortran in the 1970s and 1980s), there were very good parametric rules for estimating the time to write programs and also for estimating the cost. You can Google this, but back at that time, programmers only produced 5 to 10 lines of usable code per day! A fairly typical application of that time could encompass 100,000 lines of code or more. Even if we had 10 programmers working on the application (as many companies did back at that time), it could still take more than a year to create the application as we see from using our parametric model. This parametric model for estimating time also got translated into a parametric model for estimating cost. The parametric model for cost was that each line of code cost $10. Therefore, that application of 100,000 lines of code cost $1 million. This was a fairly typical cost estimate for companies developing their own homegrown applications at the time.

The last of the four estimating methods mentioned in the *PMBOK® Guide* is *Three-Point Estimating.* If I ask a programmer to give me an estimate for writing a new program and the programmer tells me 14 days, he's just given me his "realistic" or "most likely" estimate. I would be much better off if I also got two more estimates from the programmer: an "optimistic estimate" and also a "pessimistic estimate." I then combine these estimates using one of the three-point estimating equations: either the program evaluation and review technique (PERT[6]) equation or the triangular equation. Here are the two equations:

$$\text{PERT AVG} = (O + 4R + P)/6$$
$$\text{Triangular AVG} = (O + R + P)/3$$

---

[6] In Version Six of the *PMBOK® Guide,* PMI® no longer mentions PERT by name. Instead, they mention "Beta distributions." PERT estimates produce Beta distributions (a slightly lopsided bell-curve!), so they are still really indirectly including PERT.

(O = "optimistic"; R = "realistic"; P = "pessimistic")

For the PERT equation, we multiply "realistic" by four, or we weight the realistic value. Therefore, the PERT equation produces a "weighted" average. In the PERT equation, there are six units in the numerator, which is why we are dividing by six. PERT was first used quite successfully in the 1950s in the nuclear submarine program. Very similarly to using parametric estimating, to use three-point estimating, we need very good historical data from previous projects. As our team members are doing the three-point estimates for thousands of activities, we don't want them "winging things" and pulling the different estimates (especially the optimistic and pessimistic) out of thin air. We want these estimates to be grounded in reality. Therefore, we need the team members to compare their estimates to historical data from previous projects. Also, we need to minimize something called "anchoring." We don't want the most senior engineer in the room, or the highest paid person, to influence the estimating process and sway everyone else's opinion. Therefore, we will probably want to use the "Delphi" technique: Find a way to solicit the opinions anonymously or in such a manner that the individuals being polled are not being influenced by the other team members.

Agile Estimating Methods

Agile brings to the table several very creative and interesting estimating methods. Unfortunately, PMI® did not include these in either the *PMBOK® Guide* or the *Agile Practice Guide®*. I think these estimating methods should be part of the toolkit for all PMs. Another thing that is emphasized in many of the Agile books is the point that estimating is very difficult and most of us are quite bad at doing estimating! It's very reminiscent of Mark Twain's quote, "There are lies, damned lies and statistics!" This could get translated into "There are lies, damned lies and estimates!" or "There are lies, damned lies and models!" Especially, for our software projects and "knowledge work projects," we are dealing with the "Cone of Uncertainty." There will be so much volatility and change in our project that it will be very difficult to forecast more than a few months into the future.

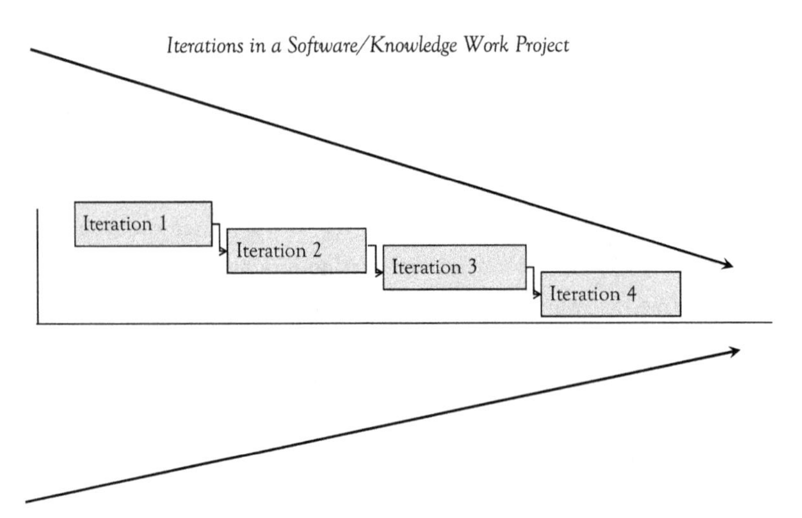

Figure 3.3 The Cone of Uncertainty

On an Agile project, we go through a number of different stages: Feasibility (or Envisioning), Initiation, Release Planning, Iteration Planning, and Daily Planning. More planning is typically done on an Agile project than in the traditional world using waterfall (Figure 3.4 and 3.5).

We use different estimating methods in these different stages and these estimating approaches are different than the methods described in the *PMBOK® Guide.*

In the *Initiation Stage*, we will obtain high-level estimates using techniques like "Affinity Estimating" or "T-Shirt Sizing." Both of these techniques are used to obtain initial high-level or coarse-grained estimates, much like the estimates we obtained with Analogous Estimating. With

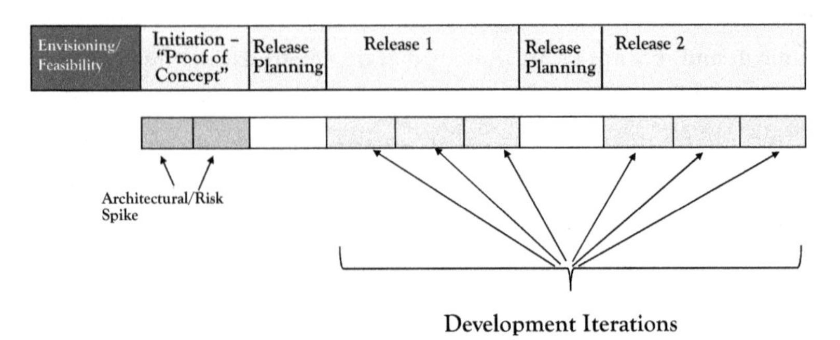

Figure 3.4 Agile development stages (phases)

Affinity Estimating, the product owner will describe all the stories and features in the Product Backlog. The team will ask the product owner questions about the different features and stories, recording the features and stories on Post-it notes or sticky notes. The Post-it notes will be stuck to the wall in the meeting room, and the team will arrange and group the Post-it notes according to the perceived weights or sizes of the stories and features. The team is not arranging the stories and features by perceived estimates of durations, but instead by their relative size or weight. T-shirt sizing is very similar. The team now puts the features and stories into different columns according to T-shirt sizes: XXL, XL, L, M, MS, S.

In Release Planning, we typically continue with "Relative Estimating," but try to get to a deeper level of granularity with these relative estimates. The most interesting of the methods for getting relative estimates, and which is used in Release Planning, is "Planning Poker."

Each team member is given a small deck of cards typically using the Fibonacci series of numbers:

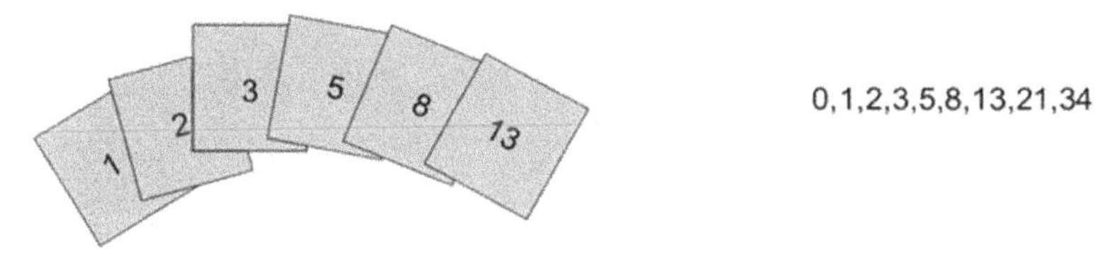

The facilitator (usually the product owner or Scrum Master) will read a story with a team discussion following each story. The product owner then answers any questions about the story.

- Each team member gives a *relative estimate* of the size of the story.
- The facilitator counts to three, and at the count of three, each team member lays down a card to indicate their relative estimate of the size of the story. (This incorporates the Delphi technique.)
- The team member who has the highest estimate explains why they rated the story at the value they did, and likewise, the team member with the lowest rating explains their evaluation.
- Successive rounds are played until the relative ratings converge to the same value.

Again, the estimates the team is coming up with here are "relative estimates," not duration estimates. Of course, eventually, we will want duration estimates for these different stories and features. How do we get these? As Mike Cohn describes in *Agile Estimating and Planning,* we can do a translation of relative estimates into duration estimates once the team has finished a couple of iterations. At this time, we will see the actual durations for the different stories and features and will be able to measure the "velocity" of the team. This allows us to translate the relative estimates into duration estimates for future iterations.

An interesting thing that *Planning Poker* is building into the estimating process is the Delphi technique. In the way that *Planning Poker* is being used, team members are not able to unduly influence the others as they are making their estimates. This is a good thing! It's also quite odd, I think, that PMI® removed all mention of the Delphi technique from Version Six. This was always one of the favorite tools–techniques for obtaining estimates and expert judgment. I find it surprising that PMI® has entirely removed it from Version Six.

Once the team gets into iteration planning, they are only looking out one to four weeks into the future. For stories that are occurring on such a near horizon, they should be able to estimate actual elapsed times for the different stories, and these estimates should be quite reliable.

Risk Management

In many places in earlier sections of this book, we've made it abundantly clear that successfully managing projects is closely intertwined with successfully handling key risks on our projects. Doing risk management well is absolutely necessary. I think this point of view is completely consistent with the traditionalists' view, the PMI® view, and also the view of the Agile community. If we don't do risk well, there is no way we can be proactive, and there's no way we can issue the favorite type of change request mentioned in the *PMBOK® Guide*: "Preventive Change Requests."

In Chapter 1, we've already discussed how Agile helps us solve four or more key risks on projects:

- The #1 Risk: a poorly written scope statement
- Allowing half-baked ideas to survive (not doing kill-points well)
- Handling impossible constraints (the impossible project)
- Not doing communications well (not keeping our sponsor, other senior managers, the customer, and other key stakeholders properly updated on the status and progress for the project). What does management hate above all else? Surprises! Negative surprises. But we must also keep them informed of good things happening with the project too. "Out of sight is out of mind," and if we haven't kept our sponsor informed of the progress we are making, and the good things we are doing, and she has not heard from us in several weeks, then other priorities might have come up. She might decide to reduce funding for our project, so she can move resources and money to something else that seems more urgent now.

In 2003, I was the VP of programs for PMIWDC. At that time, someone from Rita Mulcahy's company contacted the chapter and said Rita would be in the Washington DC area teaching a class and giving other presentations. They asked if there was any opening in our calendar where Rita could speak at one of our events. Rita was tremendously popular: she was really the first one to come out with a PMP® prep book, per se. Even though we had scheduled speakers for our dinner meetings for the next 12 months, I wanted very much to find a spot for Rita to speak. We were able to rearrange things and get her scheduled to speak at one of our upcoming dinner meetings. Rita knocked the doors down! The average attendance at our dinner meetings at that time was around 200 people. For Rita's presentation, more than 400 people showed up, taxing our capabilities to the limit and the hotel's capabilities to support that size of a crowd.

If you have read her PMP® prep book, you know Rita likes to challenge you, get right in your face, and say things like "Did you read that carefully?"—"Did you really understand?"—"If you did not, you are not really ready to be a PMP®!" I had no idea, but she was very much the same way in person at her presentation. Many speakers at our dinner meetings challenge the audience with tough questions, but they always wait for some brave soul to raise their hand, and they will pick out a member of the audience to answer the question. Not Rita! Rita would go right up to a person in the audience and say, "You look like a PMP®!"—"What would you do in this situation?" And then, she would describe a tough problem, perhaps a problem reminiscent of the types of questions on the PMP® exam!

One of the questions she posed to an audience member that evening went something like this:

> As one of the senior PMs in your company, you were just recently assigned to take over a project that was in crisis, and to get the project back on the baselines, and back on track. You are quite gifted as a PM, and you've been able to accomplish those goals. You and the team implemented corrective change requests that brought the project back on plan. However, now in the past two weeks, three different crises have popped up again, but being very gifted with your soft skills and people skills, you were able to put out these fires and handle these escalations.

She then asked this audience member, "So, what type of PM are you, and are you ready to be a PMP®?" What answer was she looking for that evening? My job in a past life at Hewlett-Packard was managing hot sites, or what we called escalations. From my vantage point as an escalation manager, I was thinking this PM had done a pretty good job solving the escalations. Was that the answer Rita was looking for that evening? No! What type of manager was the PM in this example? A reactive PM. They successfully handled these crises, but if they were really on their game, and in Rita's mind, worthy of the PMP® certification, these escalations would not have occurred. The PM would have seen the triggers of these risks about to occur and would've taken steps to mitigate or avoid these risks. In her mind, the PM needed to grow and learn risk management skills much better to be worthy of the PMP® certification.[7]

Therefore, risk management is absolutely fundamental and necessary. It is not something that we just do up front at the beginning of the project, and then we are done with it. It is something that we revisit continuously throughout the project in a very iterative manner. We are always checking to make sure we didn't miss any risks when we did the process *Identify Risks.* We are always checking to make sure we rated the risks properly in the process *Perform Qualitative Risk Analysis*, and we are always checking to make sure our response strategies are working effectively. Again, all these things are being done continuously in a very iterative way throughout the project.

How does Agile help us in this effort? It helps us because we are speeding up the PDCA loop used in iterations, and we are producing tangible, empirical results in all of our iterations. "If a picture is worth a thousand words, a prototype is worth a thousand pictures." This is exactly what we are doing in Agile by producing empirical, tangible results (product increment) in each iteration. We are grooming the value chain from iteration to iteration; we are removing waste and features that do not have value, and this is closely aligned with reducing negative risk.

Risk management helps us with what we are doing in all the other KAs described in the *PMBOK® Guide*. It helps us in the requirements

---

[7] In the *Integration Management* Chapter in the *PMBOK® Guide,* for the process *Monitor and Control Project Work,* PMI® describes three types of change requests: *Corrective Actions, Preventive Actions,* and *Defect Repairs.* A "Corrective Action" is all about fixing the project, and getting it back on plan. If there is variance, and our project has strayed away from one or more of the four baselines, a corrective action is issued to get the project back on plan, and back on the baselines. On the other hand, a "Defect Repair" is a change request to fix a deliverable that is not meeting the scope or quality requirements. Of the three types of change requests a "Preventive Action" is the best type of change request to issue! This is issued when the PM sees a negative risk that could cause variance, and the change request is issued proactively to avoid, mitigate, or transfer the negative risk before it harms the project. In our example, the PM was reactive, and fixed the problems after the variance had occurred. They issued a "Corrective Action." It would have been much better if, instead, they had issued a "Preventive Change Request."

gathering process, it helps us do prioritization better, it helps us achieve quality, it helps us communicate better, and it helps us reduce cost. Risk management is also helping us accomplish all the work occurring in other KAs by ensuring:

- We don't miss any requirements.
- The scope statement is well written and the acceptance criteria for deliverables are SMART (specific, measurable, agreed or acceptable, realistic, and time-bound).
- Improved duration and cost estimates.
- The PM Plan is complete and well written.
- Other project documents are complete and well written.
- The schedule baseline and cost baseline are appropriately protected with contingency reserves.

In Agile, we are not trying to do "predictive planning" and we don't have "defined scope" that the EVM people require. So, most of the points above are not goals in Agile.

However, there are some other disconnects between the way risk management is handled in traditional project management and the way it is handled with Agile. The disconnects mostly involve the classic documents used in traditional risk management. The Agilists don't mention tracking risks in a Risk Register or using an RBS to ensure we don't miss any risks. They also don't mention creating a Risk Management Plan to provide instructions for how we will do all the other processes in risk. (In Version Six, there are five planning processes, one executing process, and one monitoring and controlling process in Risk Management. The Risk Management Plan will define who will be involved in each process, how long the different processes will take, what will they cost, and what approach will be used for each process.)

The Agilists integrate risks into the product backlog and create a "Risk Adjusted Backlog." However, I think it makes sense to track risks separately in their own document: the Risk Register. In the Risk Register, for each risk, at minimum we will create a(n):

- Unique identifier
- Description of the risk
- Owner

- Trigger
- Category in the RBS to which the risk belongs
- Probability
- Impact
- Score
- Response strategy:
  - Fallback plan
  - Contingency plan
  - Cost of response plan
- Contingency reserve for risk

None of these items would be tracked in the Risk Adjusted Backlog, though they seem quite important!

Another document defined in the *PMBOK® Guide* that traditionalists would stand by is the "Issue log." Risks are all about uncertain, future events. They're about probability and uncertainty. Issues, on the other hand, are all about problems and conflicts that currently exist. Once a risk occurs, it is no longer a risk, it is now an "Issue." So, we want to track the current problems the project team is dealing with in an "Issue log." Minimum data items we want to track for Issues include a(n):

- Description of the issue
- Owner
- Due date
- Status
- Action plan for issue (owner typically implements the action plan).

As stated earlier, a new and interesting concept that is employed in Agile for risk management—and something that should be added to the tools–techniques in *Identify Risks*—is the use of "risk spikes." Again, these are a special experiment or an iteration to test the probability of a threat (negative risk) occurring, and reduce that probability. Similarly, "architectural spikes" are also used with Agile, and these are usually a special iteration or test of a hardware configuration, a software solution, or a design approach. For example, we may want to test different learning management solutions to see which will best meet our needs, and for the best price. These experimental and empirical tests help reduce risk by quickly running the experiments early in the project lifecycle.

The last point I would like to make here is that PMI® has a separate certification for Risk Management and that is the PMI-RMP® ("PMI Risk Management Professional") certification. I believe a PMP® certified PM should know all the materials covered on the PMI-RMP® test and be able to pass this test. Why not? What would be something special and extra that is covered on the PMI-RMP® exam that is not something a PMP® should be expected to know?

The same is true for the PMI-ACP® (PMI Agile Certified Professional) certification. Shouldn't PMP®s know all the Agile content covered on the PMI-ACP® test? I believe the answer is Yes. I don't believe the same is true for the Scheduling Professional exam (PMI-SP® or "PMI Scheduling Professional" certification). I believe that the PMI-SP® does cover specialized knowledge that is not germane for all PMs. However, I can understand keeping all these certifications as separate certifications, so PMs who only want to specialize in Agile or Risk or Scheduling can do so, without attempting to go for the much more comprehensive and challenging PMP® certification. But it should be expected that a PMP® is accomplished in all the topics covered on the current PMP® exam, the PMI-ACP® exam, and the PMI-RMP® exam. Hopefully, if PMI® ever agrees with this point of view, they should not expect PMP®s to also earn the PMI-ACP® and PMI-RMP® certifications.

Procurement Management—Different Contract Types Defined in the *PMBOK® Guide* and Agile Contracts

An overview of the three principal contract types defined by the federal government and PMI® (FFP, Cost-Reimurbsable, and Time & Materials) is detailed in Chapter 2, in the section entitled "Agile Contracts: Can Agile Be Used with Fixed Price Contracts?" Contracts are a necessary part of following sound business practices and, therefore, a necessary part of good project management practices. Many students struggle with the questions in the Procurement Management KA on the PMP® exam, because for a lot of us, we don't have to bother too much with contract questions. We have a contracts department in our company to handle most of these problems and issues for us! We don't have to ensure that the vendor has been paid or whether the vendor has invoiced us properly according to the terms and conditions, so they can get paid; the contracts department is doing that! Again, most of us don't have to worry that all the paperwork items that support the terms and conditions are being followed precisely; the contracts department is following up on these items. But when students prepare for the PMP® exam, oftentimes, their eyes are opened to a number of these issues and the different types of contracts. This is a good thing.

As we described, in the Agile world, there is a presumption of more trust between the different parties under contract. After all, the third statement in the Agile Manifesto is "Customer collaboration over contract negotiation." We are assuming that we are in more of a Time & Materials world where the customer doesn't know exactly what they want starting out in the project, and our job is to explore and discover requirements that will provide the best solution and value for them. We said, "How can I provide you a fixed price and a fixed schedule for this project when you don't know exactly what you want?" Therefore, we are in this "Time & Materials" world of discovering what will work best in short iterations as we move through the project. But customers and senior management typically don't like a "Time & Materials" basis underpinning the entire project. Maybe they will accept that for a small piece of the project, but not for the entire project. They will always be asking, "When exactly is it that you will be done?" as well as "And, exactly how much is this project going to cost?"

Most Agile contracts are some variation of Time & Materials that will provide the customer more security and confidence that the project won't go on indefinitely and they won't need "infinitely deep pockets!"

Let's explore more of the variations of traditional fixed price contracts, cost-reimbursable contracts, and Agile contracts. Interestingly, PMI did not include any of the Agile contracts in the *PMBOK® Guide,* but they do cover some different variations in the *Agile Practice Guide®*.

We explained that the FFP contract is the riskiest contract type for the vendor or seller; and for cost-reimbursable contracts and T&M contracts, the customer (or buyer) has more risk. We also said that for Agile projects, the most common contract type is T&M, usually with some ceiling or constraint attached. In this chapter, we are going to explore contract types in a little more detail. Following is an overview of various contract types:

- Firm Fixed Price (FFP)
  (a) Can also be called "lump sum."
  (b) A purchase order (PO) is the simplest type of fixed price contract.
  (c) The vendor or subcontractor is bidding a fixed price for all the work called for in the Statement of Work (SOW) and is responsible for 100 percent of any cost overruns. To achieve what is called for in the SOW, a high level of specificity and detail is needed in the SOW. This implies that starting out on this contract, the customer knows what they want in detail, and they will be choosing between vendors on price (in most cases). As we said, a fixed price contract presents the highest risk contract situation for the vendor.
- Fixed Price—Economic Price Adjustment (FP-EPA)
  (a) This is a long-term (usually multiyear) fixed price contract, and this is fairly common in the U.S. federal government. This is fixed price, but the government will allow some changes (an increase) if there is a change in economic conditions (e.g., an increase in inflation or an increase in raw materials that the vendor is depending upon and had no control over).
- Fixed Price Incentive Fee (FPIF)
  (a) This is actually a hybrid contract. The first part is CPIF, but there is a cost overrun point (Point of Total Assumption, PTA) where the contract will switch into a fixed price contract, hence FPIF. The federal government and PMI® classify this contract type as a fixed price contract.
  (b) To understand FPIF, it makes sense to go through a progression of cost reimbursable contracts, and after explaining CPIF, we will have laid a good platform for understanding FPIF.
- Cost Plus Fee (CPF; fee based on actual costs) and Cost Plus Percentage of Cost (CPPC; fee based on a percentage of actual costs). CPF and CPPC are really names for the same contract type.

  (a) The fee (or profit) is based on actual costs. With CPPC, the fee is a percentage of the actual costs. Therefore, the vendor is rewarded if costs go higher, because their profit is based on actual costs; they will get a higher profit if costs go higher. This form of contract is illegal in the U.S. federal government.
- Cost Plus Fixed Fee (CPFF; fee based upfront on estimated costs).
  (a) Now, the fee is based on estimated costs; so if there is a cost overrun, the vendor isn't rewarded because of that and will not get a higher fee. The customer is picking up 100 percent of any overrun, but the vendor's profit stays the same. There are some negative ramifications for the vendor if there is a cost overrun:
    - Their profit margin is reduced.
    - Of course, they are not endearing themselves to the customer if they are constantly performing contracts with overruns.
- Cost Plus Award Fee (CPAF)
  (a) This contract type is very similar to CPFF. There is a fixed fee that the vendor will get in all situations, but on top of that, the vendor can earn an award fee or bonus. Certain performance criteria are defined, and if the vendor meets these performance criteria, they earn the bonus (award) that will be added to the fixed fee. However, the customer is solely responsible for determining whether the vendor met the criteria. In some cases, the vendor may believe they did meet the criteria for earning the bonus, but the customer disagrees and will not award any or all of the bonus. The vendor has no recourse to appeal the decision other than starting the ADR (Alternative Dispute Resolution) procedures.
- Cost Plus Incentive Fee (CPIF)
  (a) Take the CPFF contract type, but attach incentives, so if the vendor can beat the initial cost estimates and successfully deliver the products called for in the contract for less money, then the underrun will be split between the buyer and seller according to a share ratio (e.g., 80/20). The first number in the ratio is the buyer's percentage. If there is an overrun, the vendor

will be responsible for part of the overrun according to the share ratio. Usually, there is a different share ratio for overruns. In this contract type, the buyer and the seller are clearly sharing the risks. (In all contracts, both the buyer and the seller have some risk, but in this instance, the sharing of risk is more overt.) We teach for our PMP® prep classes that though this is a shared risk contract type, the buyer has more risk than the seller.

- Fixed Price Incentive Fee Contract (FPIF)—continued
  (a) Again, this is a hybrid contract that is part CPIF and part FFP. The federal government and PMI do classify it as one of the fixed price contract types. The first half of the contract is CPIF, but with an added twist. Now there is a ceiling price (maximum price) the customer will pay. If there is a cost overrun and costs reach a certain point, then the customer will hit the ceiling price, and the contract from that point on is Fixed Price (FFP). Hence, this is "Fixed Price Incentive Fee." What defines this cost overrun point? This cost overrun point is called the "Point of Total Assumption (PTA)," a cost point where, from this point on, the vendor has total assumption or is responsible for 100 percent of any additional cost overruns. The PTA equation is:
  PTA = TC + ((CP – TP)/buyer's share)
    - TC = target cost
    - CP = ceiling price
    - TP = target price
    - (target price = target cost + target profit)

  We teach for our PMP® prep classes that though this is a shared risk contract type, the seller has more risk than the buyer.
- T&M (Time and Materials; also called "Unit Price" contracts). We discussed T&M contracts at some length in Chapter 2. To recap, these are contracts where the vendor bids a fixed price for labor rates and rental rates of equipment (usually an hour or unit price) and the vendor builds profit into these rates. The customer is also charged for any other materials the vendor must purchase. This is a hybrid contract: part fixed price (the labor rates are fixed) and part cost-reim-

bursable (any extra materials needed are billed separately). The customer has much more risk than the vendor in this type of contract. This contract type is typically used for short duration engagements when the customer doesn't know exactly what they want (the deliverables are undefined), so the vendor is hired on a T&M basis.

Figure 3.5 is a very good slide we use in our PMP® prep classes that shows the risk presented to the buyer and seller in the different traditional contract types.

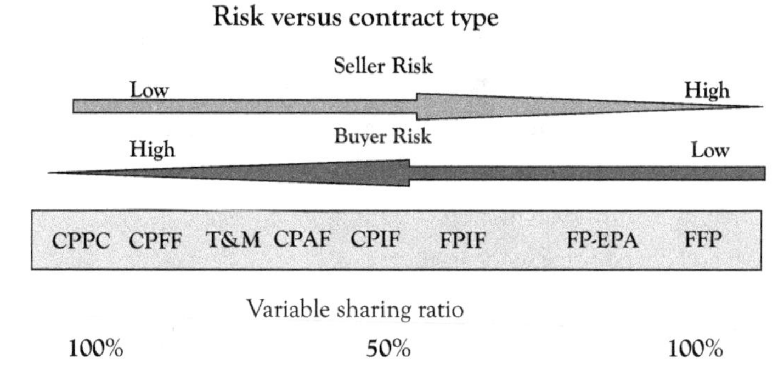

CPIF and FPIF are the two "shared risk" contract types, though both parties have risk in all contracts!

Figure 3.5 Contracts and risk

- Agile contract types. Again, the third statement of the Agile Manifesto is "Customer collaboration over contract negotiation." As they say very well in the Agile Practice Guide, "Many project failures stem from breakdowns in the customer–supplier relationship. Projects incur more risk when those involved in the contract take the perspective of winners vs. losers. A collaborative approach is one that pursues a shared-risk-reward relationship, where all sides win." [8] Therefore, with Agile contracts, the primary focus is on building trust and the buyer and seller working in a collaborative relationship. Following are some key types of Agile contracts:

[8] *Agile Practice Guide—PMI® and the Agile Alliance – p. 77*

- DSDM (Dynamic systems development method) Contract
  - (a) This contract type was commissioned by the DSDM consortium.
  - (b) In this contract, the focus is that work should be "fit for a business purpose," and on passing tests, not meeting specific design specifications.
- Time & Materials with a ceiling price
  - (a) This is simply T&M with a ceiling price or a "not to exceed" price. This builds in a natural phase-gate or kill-point decision point for the project. Once the ceiling price has been met, all work stops; the customer or product owner reviews what has been created and decides if what has been created meets their needs. If so, the project can be closed. Or perhaps the customer may decide that more work is needed, and therefore, the T&M contract will be modified and continued with a new ceiling price.
- Fixed price work-packages
  - (a) Instead of providing a detailed SOW for all deliverables for the project and a price for the entire project, the project is broken down into a number of different work-packages. The vendor then provides a fixed price estimate for the initial, high-priority work-packages to be created. As the project progresses, as new risks are being learned, and as the customer is learning better what is needed to create value, the vendor is given the leeway to re-estimate the price for new work-packages being scheduled.
- Graduated Fixed Price Contract
  - (a) In this contract type, the vendor is rewarded by being paid a higher labor rate if they beat the anticipated schedule, and conversely, they are paid a lower labor rate if the schedule

is delayed. For example, perhaps the project is planned to be made up of one-month iterations, and 10 iterations are planned. If the vendor completes the work in 10 months, their labor rate is $100 per hour; if they finish one month or more early, their labor rate will be $110 per hour; and if they finish one month or more late, their labor rate will be $90 per hour.

- "Money for Nothing and Change for Free"
  We discussed this at some length in Chapter 2 and provided an example for this type of contract. Here is what we said:
  (a) This contract type defines how we can achieve the best of the T&M world (discovering and exploring requirements in short iterations) and also give the customer and senior management the capability to do early kill-points, so they can control the price, too. Nonetheless, the vendor doing the project is protected even when an early kill-point is exercised. Here are the basics of this contract type:
  1. Customer and contractor agree on product backlog and relative weights of features/stories.
  2. During the project for any iteration (or Sprint), the customer can make any changes they want. But whatever new stories are added, then stories of equal weight are swapped out.
  3. The customer can terminate any time they want, but have to pay 20 percent of the remaining value of the project.

Where do these Agile contract types fit on the graph presented in Figure 3.5?

(a) All of the Agile contract types presented have significantly less risk for the customer than a classic T&M contract. With the exception of the DSDM contract, I believe "Time & Materials with a Ceiling Price," "Fixed Price Work-Packages," the "Graduated Fixed Price Contract," and the "Money for Nothing and Change for Free" contract have far more protection for the customer than a classic T&M contract. These contracts approach the "shared risk" contract type of CPIF.

Initial Comments on the Exposure Draft of Version Seven of the PMBOK® *Guide* and the New "Standards Plus Digital Content Platform"

In January 2020, PMI® announced they will release *PMBOK® Guide* 7th Edition in Q4 of 2020! They also released an exposure draft of the book for anyone to review and provide comments, if they so wish. They left the window open to provide comments on the exposure draft until February 14, 2020. The exposure draft is only 49 pages, and for the most part, only covers what was traditionally in the first three chapters of the *PMBOK® Guide.* I believe Version Seven will mark a tremendous departure from all previous *PMBOK® Guide* versions. Though there is very little detail in the exposure draft, it appears to be the case that PMI® will cast aside the 10 KAs and the 5 Process Groups that have essentially been the framework since Version One! The new structure that will replace the KAs and Process Groups will be "Project Delivery Principles" and a "Value Delivery System." They provide the following high-level introduction to these domains:

The Standard for Project Management—Seventh Edition provides a common basis for an understanding of project delivery. This standard applies to any project or delivery approach—such as predictive, agile, and hybrid—across industries. The standard describes the Value Delivery System, of which projects are a fundamental component. The standard identifies principles that guide the practice of project management practitioners, project team members, and other stakeholders who work on or who are engaged with projects. The principles support achievement of the intended outcomes that ultimately deliver value to organizations and stakeholders. The project delivery principles in this standard represent a departure from what has historically been a process-oriented approach to a principles-oriented approach that supports any type of project delivery. The principles articulated in this standard provide guidance for practitioner behaviors and actions for any projects and project-related activities. These principles support project teams to enable realization of the intended value from projects to the organization and stakeholders. In the context of The Standard for Project Management, project management encompasses the application of knowledge, skills, tools, and techniques to project activities to meet project requirements. While this tactical focus ensures the project delivers its intended results, this standard expands the term to address the continuing pace of change in global business. The expanded term project delivery complements the term project management. It embraces the broadening continuum of ways in which project results can be achieved by bringing a sharper focus on project outcomes rather than just project deliverables. This standard speaks to both project management and project delivery.

January 15, 2020 Exposure Draft—The Standard for Project Management—7th Edition

In recent months, they have also referenced an important new platform that will be coming out in Q2 of 2020, the "The Standards Plus Digital Content Platform." They say the following about the Standards Plus Platform:

> The Standards Plus™ interactive digital content platform presents detailed information about current, emerging and future practices, methods, artifacts and other useful information. The digital content better reflects the dynamic nature of the project management body of knowledge. It provides project practitioners and other stakeholders with access to a richer and broader range of information and resources that can more quickly accommodate advances and changes in project delivery. It explains how specific practices, tools, methods or outputs apply within projects based on industry segments, project types or other characteristics.
>
> Starting with the inputs, tools, techniques and outputs from the *PMBOK® Guide*—Sixth Edition, Standards Plus will incorporate new resources that support continued evolution in project delivery on a continuous basis.
>
> The Standards Plus platform is scheduled to launch in Q2–2020.

On the PMI® website (http://pmi.org), they provide a glimpse of what the Standards Plus Platform will contain, and how the old framework of 10 KAs and 5 Process Groups will map into the new domains.

Figures 3.6 and 3.7, respectively, are the maps of KAs and Process Groups in Version Six to the new structure in Version Seven.

So, we all need to be patient and not judge things prematurely! PMI® has given us very little with the Exposure Draft. It is really very brief and very high level. The preview of the Standards Plus Content Platform is more interesting and provides a hint of huge changes to come.

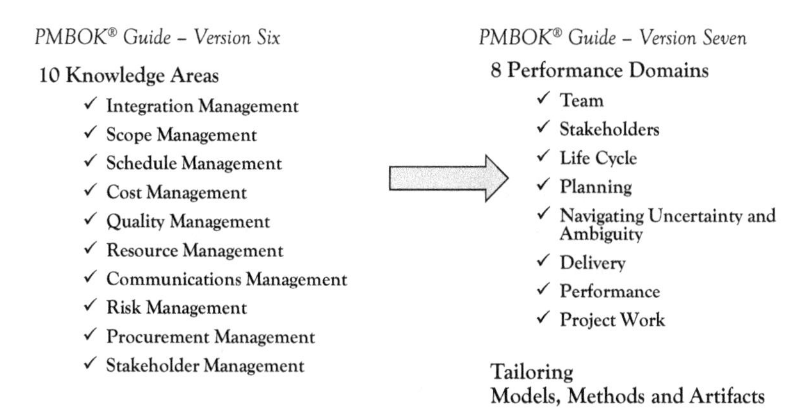

Figure 3.6 Mapping Knowledge Areas in Version Six to new structure in Version Seven

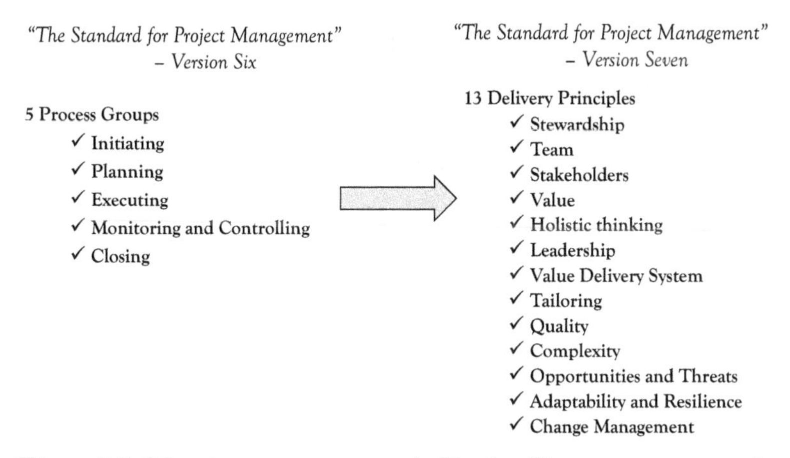

Figure 3.7 Mapping process groups in Version Six to new structure in Version Seven

From what we see in the Standards Plus Content Platform, the 10 current KAs apparently will be replaced by "Performance Domains," and there are 8 of these:

- Team
- Stakeholders
- Life Cycle
- Planning
- Navigating Uncertainty and Ambiguity

- Delivery
- Performance
- Project Work

Are these a good replacement for the current 10 KAs? Do they demarcate key areas of work that all PMs must focus on, and are these areas comprehensive and complete? My initial reaction is that I don't see it. I see some of these domains mapping into processes in current KAs, but this doesn't strike me as a complete list of concepts and KAs that project managers need to be up-to-speed on. Much is missing (focusing on Requirements, defining Scope and Quality, Integration, Communications, balancing tradeoffs between the "Triple Constraints," ensuring the project aligns with Program objectives and Strategic goals, etc.) There also seems to be some overlap and redundancy (e.g., Life Cycle and Planning; Delivery and Project Work).

It also looks like the 5 Process Groups will be replaced by "Project Delivery Principles," and it looks like there will be 13 delivery principles:

- Stewardship
- Team
- Stakeholders
- Value
- Holistic thinking
- Leadership
- Value Delivery System
- Tailoring
- Quality
- Complexity
- Opportunities and Threats
- Adaptability and Resilience
- Change Management

Obviously, these do not function at all like the five Process Groups did. So, how do these work exactly, and how do they work with the domains? Are they "principles" to guide project managers or key focus areas within the Performance Domains above? Why are these "Delivery

Principles" separated from the Performance Domains? There is overlap and commonality between the domains and the principles ("Stakeholders" appear in both; Risk concepts—"Navigating Uncertainty and Ambiguity" and "Opportunities and Threats"—appear in both).

Aren't the traditional, current KAs still important? Aren't they really a framework behind these domains and principles? Aren't the 10 KAs a simpler construct and a good foundation to guide project managers?[9] There is nothing new in either the domains or the principles. Both the domains and principles cover concepts that have always been emphasized in the *PMBOK® Guide* and in sound project management practices. "Project Management is project management," and there are no new key revelations here. PMI® is just "slicing and dicing" things differently, reorganizing and emphasizing things differently. Instead of emphasizing KAs and processes, we'll emphasize core principles, but we have always focused on these principles. As we all remember, Project Management 101 classes teach that PMs have to focus on the "5 Ws": who, what, why, when, where. (Also, "H" or "How" gets added into the mix too.) The framework is:

- **W**hat are we going to accomplish?—*Collect Requirements, Define Scope, Create WBS, Plan Quality*
- **W**hy are we doing the project?—*Develop Charter*
- **W**hen will work take place?—(All the *Scheduling* planning processes)

9 The 10 KAs are:
Integration Management
- Scope Management
- Schedule Management
- Cost Management
- Quality Management
- Resource Management
- Communications Management
- Risk Management
- Procurement Management
- Stakeholder Management

The five Process Groups are: Initiating, Planning, Executing, Monitoring & Controlling, and Closing

- ***W***ho is going to do the work?—(*Resource Management* processes)
- ***W***here is the work taking place?—(*Scope* planning processes and *Scheduling* planning processes)
- ***H***ow much will the project cost?—(*Cost Management* planning processes). Perhaps also, ***H***ow is the work occurring?—*Cost Planning* processes and *Create WBS & Define Activities*

Don't these 5 Ws map quite nicely onto the existing 10 KAs? Isn't this a much simpler, compelling, and understandable framework? Don't the 13 principles fit within this framework and support the framework? I think the answers to these questions are a loud and resounding, Yes!

Will the rest of world adopt the new Version Seven framework and replace the old KAs and Process Groups with this new framework? The current ISO-21500 standard aligns with the 10 KAs. Will ISO modify their standard? I'm doubtful that will happen. No, I believe most real-world project managers will still refer to the current KAs and Process Groups far into the future. The new principles support this framework. Many of the Version Seven principles support key topics in multiple KAs. Creating Value and having a "Value Delivery System" is key for Quality and also key for Scope. As we've described in multiple places in this book, using Lean is a huge part of creating Value and using the PDCA loop. As we've also said multiple times, the five Process Groups are an evolutionary adaptation of the PDCA loop.

What do our customers and our senior managers care most about? Do they care whether, as project managers, we are focusing on KAs and processes, or we are focusing on Principles? I think not! They want the answers to the 5 Ws! They especially want to know "What are we going to create?" "How much is this going to cost?" "When will we be finished?" Right now, I can't imagine convincing a senior manager (especially someone like the CFO) that I knew what I was doing by laying out this new framework, and saying the project team had the new inspiration to start focusing on principles instead of processes. I can see her cutting me off before I was three minutes into my sales pitch and ask, "So, Mark, when is this project going to be done?" "How much is it going to cost?" "How soon will I start seeing something of value?" and so on ...

The Agile methodologies fit easily within the "5 Ws framework" and the 10 KAs. In the "Feasibility Stage" or "Envisioning Stage," the Sponsor and product owner are focusing on "Why." This is *Develop Charter.* In the next "Initiation Stage," the key focus is creating the Product Backlog, or defining "What." This is, of course, *Collect Requirements.* The team then starts getting high-level, initial estimates, and this helps the product owner and the team do prioritization. This is *Develop Charter* at the beginning of the project, and then later *Define Scope* (define boundaries and exclusions). Next, they define initial ideas on how long the project will take (what is the Release time frame and how many iterations will be required?) Then, they progressively elaborate and go into more and more detail as they go through Release Planning, Iteration Planning, and Daily Planning. As they progressively elaborate, they are focusing very much on all of the "13 Project Management Delivery Principles" listed in Version Seven, but these principles support the methodology; they are not the framework or the methodology itself.

As we've said previously, the current *PMBOK® Guide* is not meant to be a methodology of how to do a project. Instead, it is intended to be a framework that supports all methodologies in all industries for all contract types. This is one of the principal reasons it is such a dry and cryptic book! One of the main attractions of Agile is that it is intended to be methodology, and its practitioners find it quite easy to understand and easy to use. The exposure draft for Version Seven doesn't appear to address this issue at all. By replacing a "process oriented approach" with a "principles oriented approach" PMI® is not helping project managers by providing them a good methodology (or set of methodologies) that are easy to use and easy to understand. I'm afraid PMI® will only push project managers to finding other resources for helping them manage and handle their projects.

So, again, we all need to be patient; perhaps I'm jumping the gun and making inferences that are incorrect. We all need to wait until next fall (fall of 2020) when Version Seven is formally released. I will provide an update for this chapter at that time.

Final Thoughts and Summary

We do indeed live in an "Age of Accelerations" with tremendous volatility, intense global competition, and tremendous pressure on companies to address the changing needs and demands of their customers. Therefore, there is a lot of pressure on project managers and program managers to help their companies survive in this environment. Project managers are the "Agents of Change!" Also, a huge percentage of our projects today are projects involving design work, intellectual work, and software; these are "Knowledge Work" projects. The key project management approach that applies best in this new age is Agile.

For Agile to work, the company must provide the right culture: a culture that provides significant freedom and trust to the project team members to creatively explore the solutions that will work and provide value. But Agile is not just a special set of tools and a special methodology that applies to projects and project team members. Agile is a mindset and a cultural shift. The Agile culture is not just a special culture and environment for the projects using Agile. This culture must be accepted and understood by the entire organization. Senior managers need an education and an understanding of Agile, at least at a basic level! They must understand the importance of Agile, its uses, and its value to the organization. More importantly, senior managers must understand they have a key role to play in the success of using Agile and that they must interact with the projects on a far more frequent basis than they would with a traditional project. Other managers and other employees in the organization must understand this too.

We said that traditional, waterfall approaches still have a key role to play in modern organizations today. The waterfall approach is not a thing of the past and has not been replaced by Agile. Companies need to be open to the idea of using both waterfall and Agile, but as we explained, we should not attempt to use Agile and waterfall at the same time within the same portion of a project, or within the same subproject! Use a "Scrum of Scrums" concept, and keep the Agile subprojects independent of the waterfall pieces. Nevertheless, we need be open to "Hybrid Project Management." With this approach, things will get even more difficult in providing a supportive culture and environment. It's natural in a hybrid project or program that the Agilists will not understand or accept why some subprojects are being done with waterfall, and the traditional empowered and accountable project manager may not understand or accept Agile. So, the Scrum Masters need to be sent to basic project management training that covers the nuts and bolts of traditional project management, and why it is still needed in many situations today. The traditional fully accountable PM needs to have basic Agile training also, and they need to understand why it is so critical today. Senior managers and functional managers need to go to introductory training for both approaches and also obtain training in why Hybrid is needed today, what it means, and how it should be implemented.

Creating a corporate culture of freedom and trust, and empowering team members, is not going to be easy, but an Agile mindset will support us with this shift. Many companies have a very impressive mission statement or a very impressive statement of corporate values that include a number of these Agile culture concepts. However, in too many cases, these statements can become hollow statements that are not reflected in the company's actual behavior. As a company evolves over time, and multiplies in size, or merges with another large company, the original spirit and culture of the company may get lost.

It's very difficult to keep this culture and spirit—the "Agile Ethos" or "Agile Mindset"—alive and well, but it is necessary to do so. Successful companies will find a way to do this.

For Further Reading

References used for this Book

- *A Guide to the Project Management Body of Knowledge (PMBOK® Guide), Sixth edition, Project Management Institute, Inc. 2017*
- *The Agile Practice Guide®—PMI® and the Agile Alliance—2017*
- *Scrum: The Art of Doing Twice the Work in Half the Time—Jeff Sutherland*
- *PMI-ACP Exam Prep, Updated Second Edition: A Course in a Book for Passing the PMI Agile Certified Practitioner (PMI-ACP) Exam—Mike Griffiths*
- *That Used to Be Us: How America Fell Behind in the World It Invented—Thomas Friedman & Michael Mandelbaum*
- *Thank You for Being Late—Thomas Friedman*
- *Extreme Project Management—Doug DeCarlo*
- *Agile Estimating and Planning—Mike Cohn*
- *Agile Excellence for Product Managers—Greg Cohen*
- *Agile Project Management: Creating Innovative Products—Jim Highsmith*
- *Agile Project Management with Scrum—Ken Schwaber*
- *Simple Earned Value on All Projects—(Simplified Translations of the 27 EVM Criteria)—Fleming & Koppelman*
- *Identifying and Managing Project Risk: Essential Tools for Project Managers—Tom Kendrick*
- *Project Impossible—Michael Dobson*
- *The DevOps Handbook: How to Create World-Class Agility, Reliability, and Security in Technology Organizations—Gene Kim, Patrick DeBois, et al.*
- *Managers Guide to Virtual Teams. McGraw-Hill—K. Fisher and M. Fisher (2011)*

- *Reliable Software through Composite Design—Glenford Myers*
- *Ten Dumb Mistakes That Project Managers Make—Gopal Kapur (Article—see* https://scribd.com/document/88365312/0471715395-3)
- *The Six Dimensions of Project Management: Turning Constraints into Resources—Michael Dobson and Heidi Feickert*
- *The Innovators: How a Group of Hackers, Geniuses, and Geeks Created the Digital Revolution—Walter Isaacson*
- *Rita Mulcahy's PMP Exam Prep—Rita Mulcahy*
- *What Is Hybrid Agile*—https://vitalitychicago.com/blog/what-is-hybrid-agile/
- *Project Management—A Systems Approach to Planning, Scheduling, and Controlling—Harold Kerzner, PhD*
- *Martin Fowler "Continuous Integration"*—https://martinfowler.com/articles/originalContinuousIntegration.html
- *Covey, S. 2009, "The 5 Waves of Trust," Retrieved from* http://youtube.com/watch?v=HjMNWr_qqfM
- *Arnold, J. June 12, 2006. "Cisco Telepresence Demo," Retrieved from:* http://youtube.com/watch?v=0kd2SO1_kSA

About the Authors

Mark Tolbert, PMP, PMI-ACP

Mark has over 30 years of experience in IT, including 27 years at HewlettPackard. He successfully managed support programs and projects within HP Services from 1994 through 2007. The programs and projects included a large e-selling program, a multivendor support program for a large telecommunications company, data center relocation projects, and MDM (mobile device management) programs.

Since leaving HP in June 2007, Mark has been teaching PMP® Prep classes. Mark has taught for several leading education companies, including Velociteach and Edwel Programs. Mark has also taught classes for the Washington, DC PMI® Chapter (PMIWDC) over the past 15 years, and his company, Best Practices Team, is providing two of the classes for PMIWDC this year. Best Practices Team has been the preferred provider of PMP® Prep classes for the U.S. Census Bureau for the past six years.

Mark earned his PMP certification in 1995 and the PMI-ACP® certification in 2015. Mark has been very active in the PMIWDC for the past 24 years. He has served on a number of board positions for the chapter and as trustee of the chapter from 2009 through 2013.

Mark is very passionate about project management and believes adopting the best project management practices and skills is crucial to the success of enterprises today.

Mark is a long-time resident of Northern Virginia and currently lives in Annandale with his wife Linda.

Susan Parente, PMP, PMI-RMP, PMI-ACP, PSM I, CSM, SFC, CSPO, CISSP, CRISC, RESILIA, ITIL, GCLP, MS Eng. Mgmt.

Susan Parente is a project engineer, consultant, speaker, author, professor, and mentor who leads large, complex IT software implementation projects and the establishment of Enterprise PMOs. She has 24+ years of experience leading software and business development projects in the private and public sectors, including a decade of experience implementingITprojectsfortheDoDandotherfederalgovernmentagencies. Mrs. Parente has a BS in Mechanical Engineering from the University of Rochester in New York and an MS in Engineering Management from George Washington University in District of Columbia. She has numerous project management, Agile, risk management, and IT Security certifications, including PMP®, PMI-RMP®, PMI-ACP®, CSM, CSPO, PSM I, SFC, CISSP, RESILIA, CRISC, ITIL, and CGLP. She is a CMMI and ISO 9001 practitioner.

Mrs. Parente is a principal consultant at S3 Technologies, LLC. Her company's focus is on proactively managing risks, while being Agile and adaptive. S3 Technologies does this by teaming with clients, stakeholders, and vendors and using Agile practices and risk management to deliver project successes.

Mrs. Parente is also an associate professor at Post University (Waterbury, CT), adjunct professor at Montclair State University (Montclair, NJ), and instructor at University of Virginia (Charlottesville, VA). Susan trains and mentors project managers in the areas of traditional and Agile project management and risk management. She has also coauthored a book on global risk management best practices called *Global Hot Spots: How Project and Enterprise Risk Management Practices Drive Business Results around the World.*

Susan's passion for Agile project management and risk management is apparent in her teaching and writing on these topics. She speaks at professional conferences throughout the year, writes regularly on these topics, and also has a monthly Podcast, "Not a Scrumdamentalist" via Software Process and Measurement Cast (SPAMcast): http://spamcast.libsyn.com/

Index

Note: Page numbers followed by "n" refers to footnotes.

OTHER TITLES IN THE PORTFOLIO AND PROJECT MANAGEMENT COLLECTION

Timothy J. Kloppenborg, Xavier University, Editor

- *Quantitative Tools of Project Management* by David L. Olson
- *The People Project Triangle* by Stuart Copeland and Andy Coaton
- *How to Fail at Change Management* by James Marion and John Lewis
- *Core Concepts of Project Management* by David L. Olson
- *Projects, Programs, and Portfolios in Strategic Organizational Transformation* by James Jiang and Gary Klein
- *Capital Project Management, Volume III* by Robert N. McGrath
- *Capital Project Management, Volume II* by Robert N. McGrath
- *Capital Project Management, Volume I* by Robert N. McGrath
- *Executing Global Projects* by Marion and Tracey Richardson
- *Project Communication from Start to Finish* by Geraldine E. Hynes
- *The Lost Art of Planning Projects* by Louise Worsley and Christopher Worsley
- *Adaptive Project Planning* by Louise Worsley and Christopher Worsley
- *Project Portfolio Management, Second Edition* by Clive N. Enoch

CPSIA information can be obtained
at www.ICGtesting.com
Printed in the USA
BVHW032302121122
651841BV00016B/629

9 781952 538346